Enterprise Campus Design Folio
Excerpts from the Cisco Press Book,
Cisco LAN Switching

Kennedy Clark, CCIE #2175, CCSI
Kevin Hamilton, CCSI

CISCO SYSTEMS

CISCO PRESS

Cisco Press
201 West 103rd Street
Indianapolis, IN 46290 USA

Enterprise Campus Design Folio
Excerpts from the Cisco Press Book, *Cisco LAN Switching*

Kennedy Clark, Kevin Hamilton

Copyright© 2000 Cisco Press

Cisco Press logo is a trademark of Cisco Systems, Inc.

Published by:
Cisco Press
201 West 103rd Street
Indianapolis, IN 46290 USA

Printed in the United States of America 1 2 3 4 5 6 7 8 9 0

ISBN: 1-58720-008-2

Warning and Disclaimer

This book is designed to provide information about Cisco LAN switching. Every effort has been made to make this book as complete and as accurate as possible, but no warranty or fitness is implied.

The information is provided on an "as is" basis. The authors, Cisco Press, and Cisco Systems, Inc., shall have neither liability nor responsibility to any person or entity with respect to any loss or damages arising from the information contained in this book or from the use of the discs or programs that may accompany it.

The opinions expressed in this book belong to the author and are not necessarily those of Cisco Systems, Inc.

Trademark Acknowledgments

All terms mentioned in this book that are known to be trademarks or service marks have been appropriately capitalized. Cisco Press or Cisco Systems, Inc. cannot attest to the accuracy of this information. Use of a term in this book should not be regarded as affecting the validity of any trademark or service mark.

Feedback Information

At Cisco Press, our goal is to create in-depth technical books of the highest quality and value. Each book is crafted with care and precision, undergoing rigorous development that involves the unique expertise of members from the professional technical community.

Readers' feedback is a natural continuation of this process. If you have any comments regarding how we could improve the quality of this book, or otherwise alter it to better suit your needs, you can contact us through e-mail at ciscopress@mcp.com. Please make sure to include the book title and ISBN in your message.

We greatly appreciate your assistance.

Publisher	John Wait
Executive Editor	John Kane
Cisco Systems Program Manager	Jim LeValley
Managing Editor	Patrick Kanouse
Acquisitions Editor	Brett Bartow
Development Editor	Christopher Cleveland
Project Editor	Caroline Wise
Copy Editor	Kelli Brooks
Technical Editors	Tom Nosella, Jennifer DeHaven Carroll, Phil Bourgeois, Merwyn Andrade, Stuart Hamilton
Team Coordinator	Amy Lewis
Book Designer	Gina Rexrode
Cover Designer	Jeff Ehlers
Production Team	Steve Gifford
Indexer	Tim Wright

CISCO SYSTEMS

CISCO PRESS

Corporate Headquarters
Cisco Systems, Inc.
170 West Tasman Drive
San Jose, CA 95134-1706
USA
http://www.cisco.com
Tel: 408 526-4000
        800 553-NETS (6387)
Fax: 408 526-4100

European Headquarters
Cisco Systems Europe s.a.r.l.
Parc Evolic, Batiment L1/L2
16 Avenue du Quebec
Villebon, BP 706
91961 Courtaboeuf Cedex
France
http://www-europe.cisco.com
Tel: 33 1 69 18 61 00
Fax: 33 1 69 28 83 26

Americas Headquarters
Cisco Systems, Inc.
170 West Tasman Drive
San Jose, CA 95134-1706
USA
http://www.cisco.com
Tel: 408 526-7660
Fax: 408 527-0883

Asia Headquarters
Nihon Cisco Systems K.K.
Fuji Building, 9th Floor
3-2-3 Marunouchi
Chiyoda-ku, Tokyo 100
Japan
http://www.cisco.com
Tel: 81 3 5219 6250
Fax: 81 3 5219 6001

Cisco Systems has more than 200 offices in the following countries. Addresses, phone numbers, and fax numbers are listed on the Cisco Connection Online Web site at http://www.cisco.com/offices.

Argentina • Australia • Austria • Belgium • Brazil • Canada • Chile • China • Colombia • Costa Rica • Croatia • Czech Republic • Denmark • Dubai, UAE Finland • France • Germany • Greece • Hong Kong • Hungary • India • Indonesia • Ireland • Israel • Italy • Japan • Korea • Luxembourg • Malaysia Mexico • The Netherlands • New Zealand • Norway • Peru • Philippines • Poland • Portugal • Puerto Rico • Romania • Russia • Saudi Arabia • Singapore Slovakia • Slovenia • South Africa • Spain • Sweden • Switzerland • Taiwan • Thailand • Turkey • Ukraine • United Kingdom • United States • Venezuela

About the Authors

Kennedy Clark is a CCIE instructor and consultant for Chesapeake Computer Consultants, Inc. (CCCI), a Cisco training partner. As a Cisco Certified Systems Instructor (CCSI), Kennedy was one of the original Catalyst instructors for Cisco. Having focused on Catalyst and ATM switching since 1996, he has taught a wide variety of switching classes. As a consultant for CCCI, Kennedy has been involved in the design and implementation of many large, switched backbones.

Kevin Hamilton is also an instructor and consultant for Chesapeake. As a CCSI, Kevin spends most of his instructional time teaching the Cisco Catalyst and ATM courses. Prior to joining Chesapeake, Kevin worked for 11 years at Litton-FiberCom, where he designed and deployed numerous analog and digital communications systems worldwide, including Ethernet, Token-Ring, FDDI, and ATM. Kevin obtained a degree in Electrical Engineering from Pennsylvania State University.

Contents

Foreword

As campus LAN networks become more important to the mission-critical aspect of any business, the up-front choice of modular chassis switches in the wiring closet can make a dramatic difference in any company's future technology integration advantage.

The latest Cisco Systems Catalyst® 4000 and Catalyst 6000 families of modular chassis switches make this decision even easier by leveraging advances in technology and manufacturing economies to eliminate the large premium usually paid for modular chassis benefits, and delivers the same, or better, price points as competitive stackable offerings with Gigabit Ethernet.

When you are responsible for choosing the campus LAN switching infrastructure for your company's mission-critical network, consider the product families offering next-generation modular chassis solutions that will deliver the features and performance required today, and will protect you with the new features your network will require tomorrow. Be sure to consider the Catalyst 4000 and Catalyst 6000 families—the premier Cisco enterprise wiring closet and backbone solution.

Cisco Systems hopes you find the following excerpt informative and useful in understanding the ongoing convergence of technology occurring in the enterprise wiring closet. For more information about the Catalyst 4000 family of products, please visit http://www.cisco.com/go/cat4000 or for the Catalyst 6000 family of products, visit http://www.cisco.com/go/catalyst6000.

Brad Danitz
Catalyst Switch Product Manager
Cisco Systems, Inc.

This chapter covers the following key topics:

- **Why Segment LANs?**—Discusses motivations for segmenting LANs and the disadvantages of not segmenting.

- **Segmenting LANS with Repeaters**—Discusses the purpose, benefits, and limitations of repeaters in LANs.

- **Segmenting LANS with Bridges**—Discusses how bridges create collision domains and extend networks. As the foundational technology for LAN switches, this section describes the benefits and limitations of bridges.

- **Segmenting LANS with Routers**—Discusses how routers create broadcast domains by limiting the distribution of broadcast frames.

- **Segmenting LANS with Switches**—Discusses the differences between bridges and switches, and how switches create broadcast domains differently from routers.

CHAPTER 1

Segmenting LANs

As corporations grow, network administrators find themselves deep in frustration. Management wants more users on the network, whereas users want more bandwidth. To further confuse the issue, finances often conflict with the two objectives, effectively limiting options. Although this book cannot help with the last issue, it can help clarify what technology options exist to increase the number of users served while enhancing the available bandwidth in the system. Network engineers building LAN infrastructures can choose from many internetworking devices to extend networks: repeaters, bridges, routers, and switches. Each component serves specific roles and has utility when properly deployed. Engineers often exhibit some confusion about which component to use for various network configurations. A good understanding of how these devices manipulate collision and broadcast domains helps the network engineer to make intelligent choices. Further, by understanding these elements, discussions in later chapters about collision and broadcast domains have a clearer context.

This chapter, therefore, defines broadcast and collision domains and discusses the role of repeaters, bridges, routers, and switches in manipulating the domains. It also describes why network administrators segment LANs, and how these devices facilitate segmentation.

Why Segment LANs?

Network designers often face a need to extend the distance of a network, the number of users on the system, or the bandwidth available to users. From a corporate point of view, this is a good thing, because it might indicate growth. From a network administrator's point of view, this is often a bad thing, implying sleepless nights and no weekends. Even so, how does an administrator keep everyone happy while maintaining personal sanity?

A straightforward technology answer might include the deployment of a higher speed network. If users currently attach to a legacy 10 Mbps network, you could deploy a Fast Ethernet network and provide an immediate tenfold improvement in bandwidth. Changing the network infrastructure in this way means replacing workstation adapter cards with ones capable of 100 Mbps. It also means replacing the hubs to which the stations connect. The new hubs must also support the new network bandwidth. Although effective, a wholesale upgrade might be cost prohibitive.

Segmenting LANs is another approach to provide users additional bandwidth without replacing all user equipment. By segmenting LANs, the administrator breaks a network into smaller portions and connects them with some type of internetworking equipment. Figure 1-1 illustrates a before-and-after situation for segmenting networks.

Figure 1-1   *A Network Before and After Segmentation*

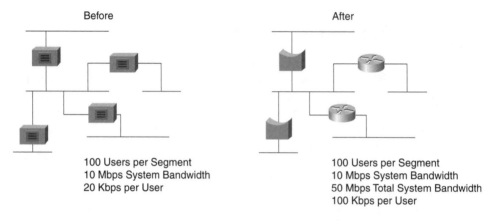

Before

After

100 Users per Segment
10 Mbps System Bandwidth
20 Kbps per User

100 Users per Segment
10 Mbps System Bandwidth
50 Mbps Total System Bandwidth
100 Kbps per User

Before segmentation, all 500 users share the network's 10 Mbps bandwidth because the segments interconnect with repeaters. (The next section in this chapter describes how repeaters work and why this is true.) The after network replaces the repeaters with bridges and routers isolating segments and providing more bandwidth for users. Bridges and routers generate bandwidth by creating new collision and broadcast domains as summarized in Table 1-1. (The sections on LAN segmentation with bridges and routers later in this chapter define collision and broadcast domains and describe why this is so.)

Table 1-1   *A Comparison of Collision and Broadcast Domain*

Device	Collision Domains	Broadcast Domains
Repeater	One	One
Bridge	Many	One
Router	Many	Many
Switch	Many	Configurable

Each segment can further divide with additional bridges, routers, and switches providing even more user bandwidth. By reducing the number of users on each segment, more bandwidth avails itself to users. The extreme case dedicates one user to each segment providing full media bandwidth to each user. This is exactly what switches allow the administrator to build.

The question remains, though, "What should you use to segment the network? Should you use a repeater, bridge, router, or LAN switch?" Repeaters do not really segment a network and do not create more bandwidth. They simply allow you to extend the network distance to some degree. Bridges, routers, and switches are more suitable for LAN segmentation. The sections that follow describe the various options. The repeater is included in the discussion because you might attach a repeater-based network to your segmented network. Therefore, you need to know how repeaters interact with segmentation devices.

Segmenting LANs with Repeaters

Legacy Ethernet systems such as 10Base5, 10Base2, and 10BaseT have distance limitations for segments as described in Chapter 1, "Desktop Technologies," of *Cisco LAN Switching*. Whenever you desire to extend the distance, you can use an internetworking device like a repeater. Repeaters operate at Layer 1 of the OSI model and appear as an extension to the cable segment. Workstations have no knowledge of the presence of a repeater which is completely transparent to the attached devices. A repeater attaches wire segments together as shown in Figure 1-2.

Figure 1-2   *Interconnecting LAN Segments with a Repeater*

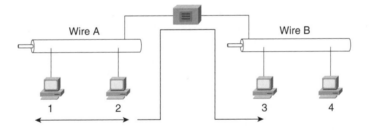

Repeaters regenerate the signal from one wire on to the other. When Station 1 transmits to Station 2, the frame also appears on Wire B, even though the source and destination device coexist on Wire A. Repeaters are unintelligent devices and have no insight to the data content. They blindly perform their responsibility of forwarding signals from one wire to all other wires. If the frame contains errors, the repeater forwards it. If the frame violates the minimum or maximum frame sizes specified by Ethernet, the repeater forwards it. If a collision occurs on Wire A, Wire B also sees it. Repeaters truly act like an extension of the cable.

Although Figure 1-2 shows the interconnection of two segments, repeaters can have many ports to attach multiple segments as shown in Figure 1-3.

Figure 1-3 *A Multiport Repeater*

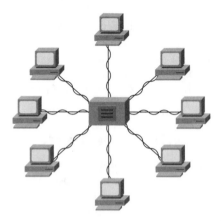

A 10BaseT network is comprised of hubs and twisted-pair cables to interconnect workstations. Hubs are multiport repeaters and forward signals from one interface to all other interfaces. As in Figure 1-2, all stations attached to the hub in Figure 1-3 see all traffic, both the good and the bad.

Repeaters perform several duties associated with signal propagation. For example, repeaters regenerate and retime the signal and create a new preamble. Preamble bits precede the frame destination MAC address and help receivers to synchronize. The 8-byte preamble has an alternating binary 1010 pattern except for the last byte. The last byte of the preamble, which ends in a binary pattern of 10101011, is called the start of frame delimiter (SFD). The last two bits indicate to the receiver that data follows. Repeaters strip all eight preamble bytes from the incoming frame, then generate and prepend a new preamble on the frame before transmission through the outbound interface.

Repeaters also ensure that collisions are signaled on all ports. If Stations 1 and 2 in Figure 1-2 participate in a collision, the collision is enforced through the repeater so that the stations on Wire B also know of the collision. Stations on Wire B must wait for the collision to clear before transmitting. If Stations 3 and 4 do not know of the collision, they might attempt a transmission during Station 1 and 2's collision event. They become additional participants in the collision.

Limitations exist in a repeater-based network. They arise from different causes and must be considered when extending a network with repeaters. The limitations include the following:

- Shared bandwidth between devices
- Specification constraints on the number of stations per segment
- End-to-end distance capability

Shared Bandwidth

A repeater extends not just the distance of the cable, but it also extends the *collision domain*. Collisions on one segment affect stations on another repeater-connected segment. Collisions extend through a repeater and consume bandwidth on all interconnected segments. Another side effect of a collision domain is the propagation of frames through the network. If the network uses shared network technology, all stations in the repeater-based network share the bandwidth. This is true whether the source frame is unicast, multicast, or broadcast. All stations see all frames. Adding more stations to the repeater network potentially divides the bandwidth even further. Legacy Ethernet systems have a shared 10 Mbps bandwidth. The stations take turns using the bandwidth. As the number of transmitting workstations increases, the amount of available bandwidth decreases.

NOTE   Bandwidth is actually divided by the number of *transmitting* stations. Simply attaching a station does not consume bandwidth until the device transmits. As a theoretical extreme, a network can be constructed of 1,000 devices with only one device transmitting and the other 999 only listening. In this case, the bandwidth is dedicated to the single transmitting station by virtue of the fact that no other device is transmitting. Therefore, the transmitter never experiences collisions and can transmit whenever it desires at full media rates.

It behooves the network administrator to determine bandwidth requirements for user applications and to compare them against the theoretical bandwidth available in the network, as well as actual bandwidth available. Use a network analyzer to measure the average and peak bandwidth consumed by the applications. This helps to determine by how much you need to increase the network's capacity to support the applications.

Number of Stations per Segment

Further, Ethernet imposes limits on how many workstations can attach to a cable. These constraints arise from electrical considerations. As the number of transceivers attached to a cable increases, the cable impedance changes and creates electrical reflections in the system. If the impedance changes too much, the collision detection process fails. Limits for legacy systems, for example, include no more than 100 attached devices per segment for a 10Base5 network. A 10Base2 system cannot exceed 30 stations. Repeaters cannot increase the number of stations supported per segment. The limitation is inherent in the bus architectures of 10Base2 and 10Base5 networks.

End-to-End Distance

Another limitation on extending networks with repeaters focuses on distance. An Ethernet link can extend only so far before the media slotTime specified by Ethernet standards is violated. As described in Chapter 1 of *Cisco LAN Switching*, the slotTime is a function of the network data rate. A 10 Mbps network such as 10BaseT has a slotTime of 51.2 microseconds. A 100 Mbps network slotTime is one tenth that of 10BaseT. The calculated network extent takes into account the slotTime size, latency through various media such as copper and fiber, and the number of repeaters in a network. In a 10 Mbps Ethernet, the number of repeaters in a network must follow the 5/3/1 rule illustrated in Figure 1-4. This rule states that up to *five* segments can be interconnected with repeaters. But only *three* of the segments can have devices attached. The other two segments interconnect segments and only allow repeaters to attach at the ends. When following the 5/3/1 rule, an administrator creates *one* collision domain. A collision in the network propagates through all repeaters to all other segments.

Figure 1-4   *Interconnecting with the 5/3/1 Rule*

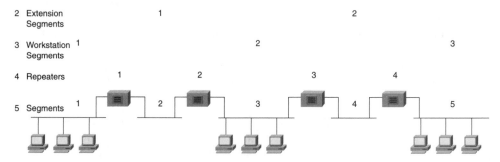

Repeaters, when correctly used, extend the collision domain by interconnecting segments at OSI Layer 1. Any transmission in the collision domain propagates to all other stations in the network. A network administrator must, however, take into account the 5/3/1 rule. If the network needs to extend beyond these limits, other internetworking device types must be used. For example, the administrator could use a bridge or a router.

Repeaters extend the bounds of broadcast and collision domains, but only to the extent allowed by media repeater rules. The maximum geographical extent, constrained by the media slotTime value, defines the collision domain extent. If you extend the collision domain beyond the bounds defined by the media, the network cannot function correctly. In the case of Ethernet, it experiences *late collisions* if the network extends too far. Late collision events occur whenever a station experiences a collision outside of the 51.2 μs slotTime.

Figure 1-5 illustrates the boundaries of a collision domain defined by the media slotTime. All segments connected together by repeaters belong to the same collision domain. Figure 1-5 also illustrates the boundaries of a broadcast domain in a repeater-based network. Broadcast domains define the extent that a broadcast propagates throughout a network.

Figure 1-5   *Broadcast and Collision Domains in a Repeater Network*

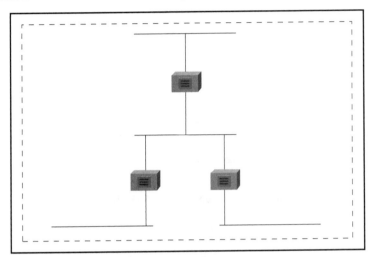

 = Collision Domain
———————————— = Broadcast Domain

To demonstrate a collision domain, consider IP's Address Resolution Protocol (ARP) process as in Figure 1-6 when IP Station 1 desires to communicate with Station 2. The stations must belong to the same subnetwork as there is no router in the network. Station 1 first ARPs the destination to determine the destination's MAC address. The ARP frame is a broadcast that traverses the entire segment and transparently passes through all repeaters in the network. All stations receive the broadcast and therefore belong to the same broadcast domain. Station 2 sends a unicast reply to Station 1. All stations receive the reply because they all belong to the same collision domain (although it is handled by the NIC hardware as discussed in Chapter 1 of *Cisco LAN Switching*).

Figure 1-6 *ARP Operation in a Repeater Network*

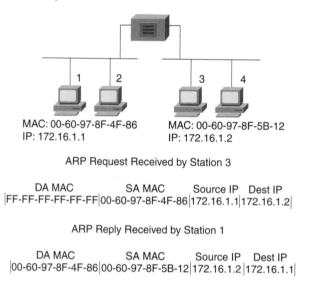

MAC: 00-60-97-8F-4F-86 MAC: 00-60-97-8F-5B-12
IP: 172.16.1.1   IP: 172.16.1.2

ARP Request Received by Station 3

DA MAC   SA MAC   Source IP   Dest IP
|FF-FF-FF-FF-FF-FF|00-60-97-8F-4F-86|172.16.1.1|172.16.1.2|

ARP Reply Received by Station 1

DA MAC   SA MAC   Source IP   Dest IP
|00-60-97-8F-4F-86|00-60-97-8F-5B-12|172.16.1.2|172.16.1.1|

Segmenting LANs with Bridges

As discussed in the previous section, Ethernet rules limit the overall distance a network segment extends and the number of stations attached to a cable segment. What do you do if you need to go further or add more devices? Bridges provide a possible solution. When connecting networks as in Figure 1-7, significant differences exist when compared to repeater-connected networks. For example, whenever stations on the same segment transmit to each other in a repeated network, the frame appears on all other segments in the repeated network. But this does not normally happen in a bridged network. Bridges use a filter process to determine whether or not to forward a frame to other interfaces.

Figure 1-7 *Interconnecting Segments with a Bridge*

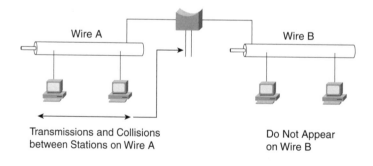

Wire A   Wire B

Transmissions and Collisions   Do Not Appear
between Stations on Wire A   on Wire B

The filter process differs for access methods such as Ethernet and Token Ring. For example, Ethernet employs a process called *transparent bridging* that examines the destination MAC address and determines if a frame should be forwarded, filtered, or flooded. Bridges operate at Layer 2 of the OSI model, the data link layer. By functioning at this layer, bridges have the capability to examine the MAC headers of frames. They can, therefore, make forwarding decisions based on information in the header such as the MAC address. Token Ring can also use source-route bridging which determines frame flow differently from transparent bridges. These methods, and others, are discussed in more detail in Chapter 3, "Bridging Technologies," of *Cisco LAN Switching*

More importantly, though, bridges interconnect collision domains allowing independent collision domains to appear as if they were connected, without propagating collisions between them. Figure 1-8 shows the same network as in Figure 1-5, but with bridges interconnecting the segments. In the repeater-based network, all the segments belong to the same collision domain. The network bandwidth was divided between the four segments. In Figure 1-8, however, each segment belongs to a different collision domain. If this were a 10 Mbps legacy network, each segment would have its own 10 Mbps of bandwidth for a collective bandwidth of 40 Mbps.

Figure 1-8   *Bridges Create Multiple Collision Domains and One Broadcast Domain*

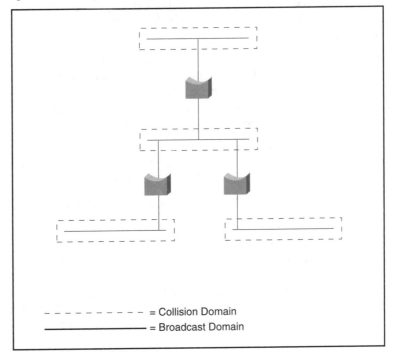

This significant improvement in bandwidth demonstrates why segmenting a LAN benefits users. The same number of users in the network in Figure 1-8 now have more available bandwidth than they did in the network in Figure 1-5. Although switching is discussed later in the chapter, it is valid to comment now that the ultimate bandwidth distribution occurs when you dedicate one user for each bridge interface. Each user then has all of the local bandwidth to himself; only one station and the bridge port belong to the collision domain. This is, in effect, what switching technology does.

Another advantage of bridges stems from their Layer 2 operation. In the repeater-based network, an end-to-end distance limitation prevents the network from extending indefinitely. Bridges allow each segment to extend a full distance. Each segment has its own slotTime value. Bridges do not forward collisions between segments. Rather, bridges isolate collision domains and reestablish slotTimes. Bridges can, in theory, extend networks indefinitely. Practical considerations prevent this, however.

Bridges filter traffic when the source and destination reside on the same interface. Broadcast and multicast frames are the exception to this. Whenever a bridge receives a broadcast or multicast, it floods the broadcast message out all interfaces. Again, consider ARP as in the repeater-based network. When a station in a bridged network wants to communicate with another IP station in the same bridged network, the source sends a broadcast ARP request. The request, a broadcast frame, passes through all bridges and out all bridge interfaces. All segments attached to a bridge belong to the same broadcast domain. Because they belong to the same broadcast domain, all stations should also belong to the same IP subnetwork.

A bridged network can easily become overwhelmed with broadcast and multicast traffic if applications generate this kind of traffic. For example, multimedia applications such as video conferencing over IP networks create multicast traffic. Frames from all participants propagate to every segment. In effect, this reduces the network to appear as one giant shared network. The bandwidth becomes shared bandwidth.

In most networks, the majority of frames are not broadcast frames. Some protocols generate more than others, but the bandwidth consumed by these protocol broadcast frames is a relatively small percentage of the LAN media bandwidth.

When should you use bridges? Are there any advantages of bridges over repeaters? What about stations communicating with unicast frames? How do bridges treat this traffic?

When a source and destination device are on the same interface, the bridge filters the frames and does not forward the traffic to any other interface. (Unless the frame is a broadcast or multicast.) If the source and destination reside on different ports relative to the bridge, the bridge forwards the frame to the appropriate interface to reach the destination. The processes of filtering and selective forwarding preserve bandwidth on other segments. This is a significant advantage of bridges over repeaters that offers no frame discrimination capabilities.

When a bridge forwards traffic, it does not change the frame. Like a repeater, a bridge does nothing more to the frame than to clean up the signal before it sends it to another port. Layer 2 and Layer 3 addresses remain unchanged as frames transit a bridge. In contrast, routers change the Layer 2 address. (This is shown in the following section on routers.)

A rule of thumb when designing networks with bridges is the 80/20 rule. This rule states that bridges are most efficient when 80 percent of the segment traffic is local and only 20 percent needs to cross a bridge to another segment. This rule originated from traditional network design where server resources resided on the same segments with the client devices they served, as in Figure 1-9.

Figure 1-9 *The 80/20 Rule Demonstrated in a Traditional Network*

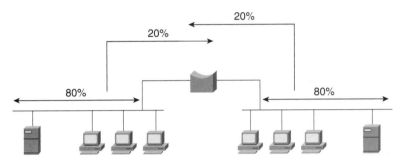

The clients only infrequently needed to access devices on the other side of a bridge. Bridged networks are considered to be well designed when the 80/20 rule is observed. As long as this traffic balance is maintained, each segment in the network appears to have full media bandwidth. If however, the flow balance shifts such that more traffic gets forwarded through the bridge rather than filtered, the network behaves as if all segments operate on the same shared network. The bridge in this case provides nothing more than the capability to daisy-chain collision domains to extend distance, but without any bandwidth improvements.

Consider the worst case for traffic flow in a bridged network: 0/100 where none of the traffic remains local and all sources transmit to destinations on other segments. In the case of a two-port bridge, the entire system has shared bandwidth rather than isolated bandwidth. The bridge only extends the geographical extent of the network and offers no bandwidth gains. Unfortunately, many intranets see similar traffic patterns, with typical ratios of 20/80 rather than 80/20. This results from many users attempting to communicate with and through the Internet. Much of the traffic flows from a local segment to the WAN connection and crosses broadcast domain boundaries. Chapter 14, "Campus Design Models," of *Cisco LAN Switching* discusses the current traffic trends and the demise of the 80/20 rule of thumb in modern networks.

One other advantage of bridges is that they prevent errored frames from transiting to another segment. If the bridge sees that a frame has errors or that it violates the media access method size rules, the bridge drops the frame. This protects the destination network from bad frames that do nothing more than consume bandwidth for the destination device discards the frame anyway. Collisions on a shared legacy network often create frame fragments that are sometimes called runt frames. These frames violate the Ethernet minimum frame size rule of 64 bytes. Chapter 3, "Bridging Technologies," of *Cisco LAN Switching* shows the frame size rules in Table 3-5. Whereas a repeater forwards runts to the other segments, a bridge blocks them.

Segmenting LANs with Routers

Bridges, operating at a layer higher than repeaters, add functionality to the network, which is not present in repeaters. Bridges perform all repeater functions, and more, by creating new collision domains. Likewise, routers, which operate at Layer 3, add functionality beyond bridges. Routers extend networks like bridges, but they create both collision and broadcast domains. Routers prevent broadcasts from propagating across networks. This broadcast isolation creates individual *broadcast domains* not found in bridges. The router behavior of blocking broadcast frames defines broadcast domain boundaries—the extent to which a broadcast frame propagates in a network. Figure 1-10 shows a network built with routers and identifies collision and broadcast domains.

Figure 1-10 *Broadcast and Collision Domains in a Routed Network*

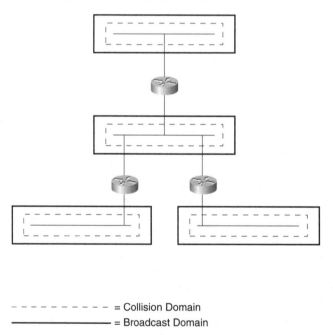

```
- - - - - - - - - - -  = Collision Domain
―――――――――――  = Broadcast Domain
```

A side effect of separate broadcast domains demonstrates itself in the behavior of routers. In a repeater- or bridge-based network, all stations belong to the same subnetwork because they all belong to the same broadcast domain. In a router-based network, however, which creates multiple broadcast domains, each segment belongs to a different subnetwork. This forces workstations to behave differently than they did in the bridged network. Refer to Figure 1-11 and Table 1-2 for a description of the ARP process in a routed network. Although the world does not need another description of ARP, it does in this case serve to illustrate how frames flow through a router in contrast to bridges and repeaters. Further, it serves as an example of how workstations must behave differently with the presence of a router. In a bridge- or repeater-based network, the workstations transmit as if the source and destination are in the collision domain, even though it is possible in a bridged network for them to be in different domains. The aspect that allows them to behave this way in the bridged network is that they are in the same broadcast domain. However, when they are in different broadcast domains, as with the introduction of a router, the source and destination must be aware of the router and must address their traffic to the router.

Figure 1-11 *Frame Header Changes through a Router*

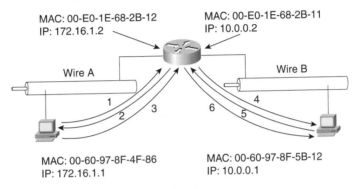

Table 1-2 *Frame Exchange in a Routed Network*

	Layer 2 Header (Modified)		Layer 3 Header (Unmodified)	
Frame	Destination MAC	Source MAC	Source IP	Destination IP
1*	FF-FF-FF-FF-FF-FF	00-60-97-8F-4F-86	172.16.1.1	172.16.1.2
2**	00-60-97-8F-4F-86	00-E0-1E-68-2B-12	172.16.1.2	172.16.1.1
3***	00-E0-1E-68-2B-12	00-60-97-8F-4F-86	172.16.1.1	10.0.0.1
4*	FF-FF-FF-FF-FF-FF	00-E0-1E-68-2B-11	10.0.0.2	10.0.0.1
5**	00-E0-1E-68-2B-11	00-60-97-8F-5B-12	10.0.0.1	10.0.0.2
6***	00-60-97-8F-5B-12	00-E0-1E-68-2B-11	172.16.1.1	10.0.0.1

*ARP Request

**ARP Reply

***User Data Frame

When Station 1 wants to talk to Station 2, Station 1 realizes that the destination is on a different network by comparing the destination's logical address to its own. Knowing that they are on different networks forces the source to communicate through a router. The router is identified through the default router or default gateway setting on the workstation. To communicate with the router, the source must address the router at Layer 2 using the router's MAC address. To obtain the router's MAC address, the source first ARPs the router (see frames 1 and 2 in Figure 1-11). The source then creates a frame with the router's MAC address as the destination MAC address and with Station 2's logical address for the destination Layer 3 address (see frame 3 in Figure 1-11). When the frame enters the router, the router determines how to get to the destination network. In this example, the destination directly attaches to the router. The router ARPs for Station 2 (frames 4 and 5 in Figure 1-11) and creates a frame with station 2's MAC address for the L2 destination and router's MAC for the L2 source (see frame 6 in Figure 1-11). The router uses L3 addresses for Stations 1 and 2. The data link layer header changes as the frame moves through a router, while the L3 header remains the same.

In contrast, remember that as the frame transits a repeater or bridge, the frame remains the same. Neither repeaters nor bridges modify the frame. Like a bridge, routers prevent errored frames from entering the destination network.

Segmenting LANs with Switches

So far, this chapter reviewed three legacy internetworking devices. These devices interconnected networks and segments together. During the early 1990s, a bridge derivative found a place in the market. Kalpana introduced a LAN switching device, called the EtherSwitch. EtherSwitch was a glorified bridge in that it offered many ports to attach directly to devices rather than to segments. Each port defined a separate collision domain providing maximum media bandwidth for the attached user. Such an innovative application of a well-known technology, bridging, quickly found favor among network administrators. It provided immediate bandwidth increase for users without needing to implement a complete infrastructure renovation. Recognizing the technology value, Cisco Systems purchased Kalpana in December of 1994. This complemented the Catalyst product line acquired in September 1993 from Crescendo Communications. The Catalyst product line consisted of the Catalyst 1200 and, in March of 1995, the Catalyst 5000. Yet another acquisition in September 1995 of Grand Junction Networks further expanded the product line by introducing the Catalyst 1900 and 2820 products. This growing product line deeply penetrated and frontiered the switching market.

What exactly is a LAN switch? A LAN switch is a multiport bridge that allows workstations to attach directly to the switch to experience full media bandwidth and enables many workstations to transmit concurrently. For example, Figure 1-12 shows four workstations communicating at the same time, something impossible in a shared network environment.

Figure 1-12 *Multiple Concurrent Sessions through a LAN Switch*

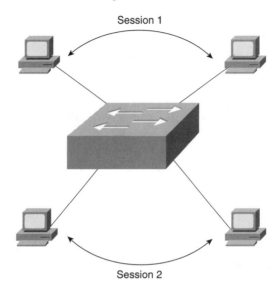

Because a switch is nothing more than a complex bridge with multiple interfaces, all of the ports on a switch belong to one broadcast domain. If Station 1 sends a broadcast frame, all devices attached to the switch receive it. The switch floods broadcast transmissions to all other ports. Unfortunately, this makes the switch no more efficient than a shared media interconnected with repeaters or bridges when dealing with broadcast or multicast frames.

It is possible to design the switch so that ports can belong to different broadcast domains as assigned by a network administrator, thus providing broadcast isolation. In Figure 1-13, some ports belong to Broadcast Domain 1 (BD1), some ports to Broadcast Domain 2 (BD2), and still others to Broadcast Domain 3 (BD3). If a station attached to an interface in BD1 transmits a broadcast frame, the switch forwards the broadcast only to the interfaces belonging to the same domain. The other broadcast domains do not experience any bandwidth consumption resulting from BD1's broadcast. In fact, it is impossible for *any* frame to cross from one broadcast domain to another without the introduction of another external device, such as a router, to interconnect the domains.

Figure 1-13 *A Multibroadcast Domain Capable Switch*

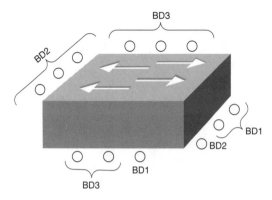

Switches capable of defining multiple broadcast domains actually define *virtual LANs* (VLANs). Each broadcast domain equates to a VLAN. Chapter 5, "VLANs," of *Cisco LAN Switching* discusses VLANs in more detail. For now, think of a VLAN capable switch as a device that creates multiple isolated bridges as shown in Figure 1-14.

Figure 1-14 *A Logical Internal Representation of a VLAN Capable Switch*

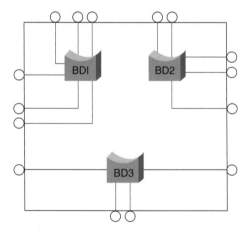

If you create five VLANs, you create five virtual bridge functions within the switch. Each bridge function is logically isolated from the others.

Summary

What is the difference between a bridge and a switch? Marketing. A switch uses bridge technology but positions itself as a device to interconnect individual devices rather than networks. Both devices create collision domains on each port. Both have the potential to create multiple broadcast domains depending upon the vendor implementation and the user configuration.

Review Questions

Refer to the network setup in Figure 1-15 to answer Questions 1 and 2.

Figure 1-15 *Graphic for Review Questions 1 and 2*

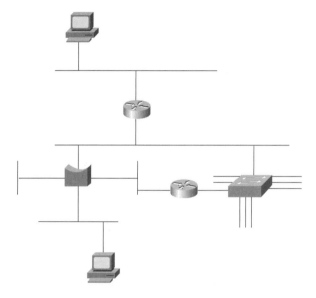

1 Examine Figure 1-15. How many broadcast and collision domains are there?

2 In Figure 1-15, how many Layer 2 and Layer 3 address pairs are used to transmit between Stations 1 and 2?

Refer to the network setup in Figure 1-16 to answer Question 3.

Figure 1-16   *Graphic for Review Question 3*

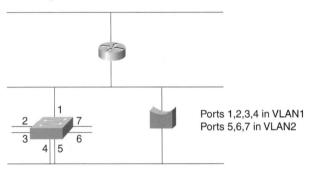

Ports 1,2,3,4 in VLAN1
Ports 5,6,7 in VLAN2

3   What is the problem with the network in Figure 1-16?

4   If you attach a multiport repeater (hub) to a bridge port, how many broadcast domains are seen on the hub?

5   Can a legacy bridge belong to more than one broadcast domain?

This chapter covers the following key topics:

- **Changing Traffic Patterns**—The rise of client/server computing, server farms, and Internet-based technology has dramatically changed most campus traffic patterns. This chapter looks at some of the challenging issues that this has created for campus network designers.

- **Campus Design Terminology**—Explains IDF/MDF and access/distribution/core terminology, the two most common ways of explaining and discussing campus designs.

- **Key Requirements of Campus Designs**—Looks at the attributes of the ideal campus design.

- **Advantages of Routing**—The recommended approach to campus design makes extensive use of Layer 3 switching (routing) technology. The important benefits of this approach are discussed.

- **Campus Design Models**—Three of the most common campus design models are discussed: the router and hub model, the campus-wide VLANs model, and the multilayer model.

- **General Recommendation: Multilayer Model**—Some specific considerations and issues associated with the multilayer model, the recommended approach to campus design, are discussed.

- **Distribution Blocks**—Discusses issues related to distribution blocks (usually a set of switches contained within a single building) for the multilayer design model.

- **Core**—Explains issues related to designing a core for a multilayer network.

CHAPTER 2

Campus Design Models

This chapter looks at several important models that can be used for campus designs. The discussion begins with a look at two sets of terminology used to describe and discuss network designs. Then, the three main approaches to campus design are presented:

- First, the traditional router and hub model is covered. Although this design is not suitable for use in modern campus networks, the proven advantages of this design are highlighted.

- Second, the chapter discusses the campus-wide VLANs or "flat earth" design. This is the design most people think of when the subject of a switched campus network comes up. Although it can be very useful for certain requirements, in general, it has many drawbacks and downsides.

- Third, the multilayer model is presented. This model is designed to blend Layer 2 and Layer 3 processing into a cohesive whole. The last half of the chapter elaborates on some issues that are specific to the multilayer architecture.

Whereas this chapter focuses on overall design architectures and paradigms, Chapter 15, "Campus Design Implementation," of *Cisco LAN Switching* looks at specific strategies associated with campus designs. For example, this chapter points out the advantages of the multilayer model for the Spanning-Tree Protocol (STP), and Chapter 15 of *Cisco LAN Switching* discusses STP best practices and makes specific STP recommendations.

Finally, please note that the intent of this chapter is not to create a survey of every campus design ever conceived. Instead, this text is oriented toward the design *process*. It explores several of the more popular and widely applicable designs in an attempt to discuss good design practices, as well as the pros and cons of various approaches to campus design.

Changing Traffic Patterns

Any effective campus design must take traffic patterns into account. Otherwise, switching and link bandwidth are almost certainly wasted. The good news is that most modern campus networks follow several trends that create unmistakable flows. This section discusses the traditional campus traffic patterns and shows how popular new technologies have drastically changed this.

The earliest seeds of today's campus networks began with departmental servers. In the mid-1980s, the growth of inexpensive PCs led many organizations to install small networks utilizing Ethernet, ArcNet, Token Ring, LocalTalk, and a variety of proprietary solutions. Many of these networks utilized PC-based server platforms such as Novell's Netware. Not only did this promote the sharing of information, it allowed expensive hardware such as laser printers to be shared.

Throughout the late-1980s, these small networks began to pop up throughout most corporations. Each network was built to serve a single workgroup or department. For example, the finance department would have a separate network from the human resources department. Most of these networks were extremely decentralized. In many cases, they were installed by non-technical people employed by the local workgroup (or outside consultants hired by the workgroup). Although some companies provided centralized support and guidelines for deploying these departmental servers, few companies provided links between these pockets of network computing.

In the early 1990s, multiprotocol routers began to change all of this. Routers suddenly provided the flexibility and scalability to begin hooking all of these "network islands" into one unified whole. Although routers allowed media-independent communication across the many different types of data links deployed in these departmental networks, Ethernet and Token Ring became the media of choice. Routers were also used to provide seamless communication across wide-area links.

Early routers were obviously extremely bandwidth-limited compared to today's products. How then did these networks function when the Gigabit networks of today strain to keep up? There are two main factors: the *quantity* of traffic and the *type* of traffic.

First, there was considerably less traffic in campus networks at the time early router-based campus networks were popular. Simply put, fewer people used the network. And those who did use it tended to use less network-intensive applications.

However, this is not to say that early networks were like a 15-lane highway with only three cars on it. Given the lower available bandwidth of these networks, many had very high average and peak utilization levels. For instance, before the rise of client/server computing, many databases utilized file servers as a simple "hard drive at the end of a long wire." Thousands of dBase and Paradox applications were deployed that essentially pulled the entire database across the wire for each query. Therefore, although the *quantity* of traffic has grown dramatically, another factor is required to explain the success of these older, bandwidth-limited networks.

To explain this difference, the *type* of traffic must be considered. Although central MIS organizations used routers and hubs to merge the network into a unified whole, most of the traffic remained on the local segment. In other words, although the networks were linked together, the workgroup servers remained within the workgroups they served. For example, a custom financial application developed in dBase needed to use only the finance department's server; it never needed to access the human resource server. The growing amount of file and printer server traffic also tended to follow the same patterns.

These well-established and localized traffic flows allowed designers to utilize the popular 80/20 rule. Eighty (or even 90+) percent of the traffic in these networks remained on the local segment. Hubs (or possibly early "switching hubs") could support this traffic with relative ease. Because only 20 (or even less than 10) percent of the traffic needed to cross the router, the limited performance of these routers did not pose significant problems.

With blinding speed, all of this began to change in the mid-1990s. First, enterprise databases were deployed. These were typically large client/server systems that utilized a small number of highly centralized servers. On one hand, this dramatically cut the amount of traffic on networks. Instead of pulling the entire database across the wire, the application used technologies such as Structured Query Language (SQL) to allow intelligent database servers to first filter the data before it was transmitted back to the client. In practice, though, client/server systems began to significantly increase the utilization of network resources for a variety of reasons. First, the use of client/server technology grew at a staggering rate. Although each query might only generate one fourth of the traffic of earlier systems, many organizations saw the number of transactions increase by a factor of 10–100. Second, the centralized nature of these applications completely violated the 80/20 rule. In the case of this traffic component, 100 percent needs to cross the router and leave the local segment.

Although client/server applications began to tax traditional network designs, it took the rise of Internet and intranet technologies to completely outstrip available router (and hub) capacity. With Internet-based technology, almost 100 percent of the traffic was destined to centralized servers. Web and e-mail traffic generally went to a small handful of large UNIX boxes running HTTP, Simple Mail Transfer Protocol (SMTP), and Post Office Protocol (POP) daemons. Internet-bound traffic was just as centralized because it needed to funnel through a single firewall device (or bank of redundant devices). This trend of centralization was further accelerated with the rise of server farms that began to consolidate workgroup servers. Instead of high-volume file and print server traffic remaining on the local wire, everything began to flow across the corporate backbone.

As a result, the traditional 80/20 rule has become inverted. In fact, most modern networks have less than five percent of their traffic constrained to the local segment. When this is combined with the fact that these new Internet-based technologies are wildly popular, it is clear that the traditional router and hub design is no longer appropriate.

TIP	Be sure to consider changing traffic patterns when designing a campus backbone. In doing so, try to incorporate future growth and provide adequate routing performance.

Campus Design Terminology

This section explains some of the terminology that is commonly used to describe network designs. The discussion begins with a review of the Intermediate Distribution Frame/Main Distribution Frame (IDF/MDF) terminology that has been borrowed from the telephone industry. It then looks at a three-level paradigm that can be very useful.

IDF/MDF

For years, the telephone industry has used the terms Intermediate Distribution Frame (IDF) and Main Distribution Frame (MDF) to refer to various elements of structured cabling. As structured cabling has grown in popularity within data-communication circles, this IDF/MDF terminology has also become common.

The following sections discuss some of the unique requirements of switches placed in IDF and MDF closets. In addition to these specialized requirements, some features should be shared across all of the switches. For new installations, all of the switches should offer a wide variety of media types that include the various Ethernet speeds and ATM. FDDI and Token Ring support can be important when migrating older networks. Also, because modern switched campus infrastructures are too complex for the "plug-it-in-and-forget-it" approach, comprehensive management capabilities are a must.

IDF

IDF wiring closets are used to connect end-station devices such as PCs and terminals to the network. This "horizontal wiring" connects to wall-plate jacks at one end and typically consists of unshielded twisted-pair (UTP) cabling that forms a star pattern back to the IDF wiring closet. As shown in Figure 2-1, each floor of a building generally contains one or more IDF switches. Each end station connects back to the nearest IDF wiring closet. All of the IDFs in a building generally connect back to a pair of MDF devices often located in the building's basement or ground floor.

Figure 2-1   *Multiple IDF Wiring Closets*

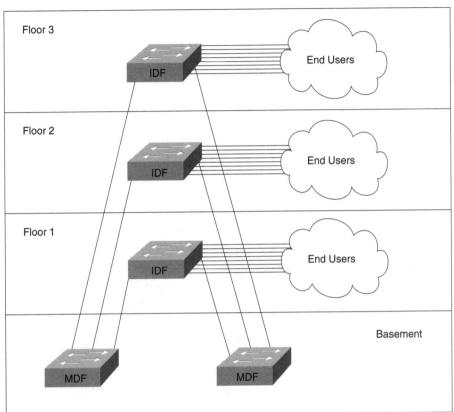

Given the role that they perform, IDF wiring closets have several specific requirements:

- **Port density**—Because large numbers of end stations need to connect to each IDF, high port density is a must.

- **Cost per port**—Given the high port density found in the typical IDF, cost per port must be reasonable.

- **Redundancy**—Because several hundred devices often connect back to each IDF device, a single IDF failure can create a significant outage.

- **Reliability**—This point is obviously related to the previous point, however, it highlights the fact that an IDF device is usually an end station's only link to the rest of the world.

- **Ease of management**—The high number of connections requires that per-port administration be kept to a minimum.

Because of the numerous directly connected end users, redundancy and reliability are critical to the IDF's role. As a result, IDFs should not only utilize redundant hardware such as dual Supervisors and power supplies, they should have multiple links to MDF devices. Fast failover of these redundant components is also critical.

IDF reliability brings up an interesting point about end-station connections. Outside of limited environments such as financial trading floors, it is generally not cost-effect to have end stations connected to more than one IDF device. Therefore, the horizontal cabling serves as a single point of failure for most networks. However, note that these failures generally affect only one end station. This is several orders of magnitude less disruptive than losing an entire switch. For important end stations such as servers, dual-port network interface cards (NICs) can be utilized with multiple links to redundant server farm switches.

The traditional device for use in IDF wiring closets is a hub. Because most hubs are fairly simple devices, the price per port can be very attractive. However, the shared nature of hubs obviously provides less available bandwidth. On the other hand, routers and Layer 3 switches can provide extremely intelligent bandwidth sharing decisions. On the downside, these devices can be very expensive and generally have limited port densities.

To strike a balance between cost, available bandwidth, and port densities, almost all recently deployed campus networks use Layer 2 switches in the IDF. This can be a very cost-effective way to provide 500 or more end stations with high-speed access into the campus backbone.

However, this is not to say that some Layer 3 technologies are not appropriate for the wiring closet. Cisco has introduced several IDF-oriented features that use the Layer 3 and 4 capabilities of the NetFlow Feature Card (NFFC). As discussed in Chapter 5, "VLANs," and Chapter 11, "Layer 3 Switching," of *Cisco LAN Switching*, Protocol Filtering can be an effective way to limit the impact of broadcasts on end stations. By allowing a port to only output broadcasts for the Layer 3 protocols that are actually in use, valuable CPU cycles can be saved. For example, a broadcast-efficient TCP/IP node in VLAN 2 can be spared from being burdened with IPX SAP updates. IGMP Snooping is another feature that utilizes the NFFC to inspect Layer 3 information. By allowing the Catalyst to prune ports from receiving certain multicast addresses, this feature can save significant bandwidth in networks that make extensive use of multicast applications. Finally, the NFFC can be used to classify traffic for Quality of Service/Class of Service (QoS/COS) purposes.

TIP   The most important IDF concerns are cost, port densities, and redundancy.

MDF

IDF devices collapse back to one or more Main Distribution Frame (MDF) devices in a star-like fashion. Each IDF usually connects to two different MDF devices to provide adequate redundancy. Some organizations place both MDF devices in the same physical closet and rely on disparate routing of the vertical cabling for redundancy. Other organizations prefer to place the MDF devices in separate closets altogether. The relationship between buildings and MDFs is not a hard rule—larger buildings might have more than two MDF switches, whereas a pair of redundant MDF devices might be able to carry multiple buildings that are smaller in size.

Figure 2-2 shows three buildings with MDF closets. To meet redundancy requirements, each building generally houses two MDF devices. The MDF devices can also be used to interconnect the three buildings (other designs are discussed later).

Figure 2-2   *MDF Closets*

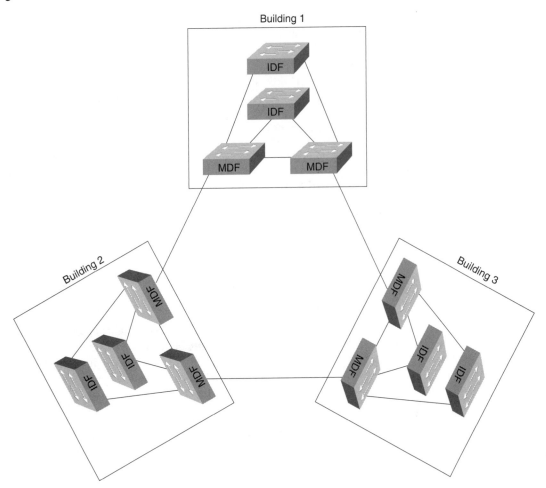

MDF closets have a different set of requirements and concerns than IDF closets:

- Throughput
- High availability
- Routing capabilities

Given that they act as concentration points for IDF traffic, MDF devices must be able to carry extremely high levels of traffic. In the case of a Layer 2 switch, this bandwidth is inexpensive and readily available. However, as is discussed later in this chapter, many of the strategies to achieve robust and scalable designs require routing in the MDF. Achieving this level of Layer 3 performance can require some careful planning. For more information on Layer 3 switching, see Chapter 11 of *Cisco LAN Switching*. Issues associated with Layer 3 switching are also addressed later in this chapter and in Chapter 15 of *Cisco LAN Switching*.

High availability is an important requirement for MDF devices. Although the failure of either an MDF or IDF switch potentially affects many users, there is a substantial distinction between these two situations. As discussed in the previous section, the failure of an IDF device completely disables the several hundred attached end stations. On the other hand, because MDFs are almost always deployed in pairs, failures rarely result in a complete loss of connectivity. However, this is not to say that MDF failures are inconsequential. To the contrary, MDF failures often affect thousands of users, many more than with an IDF failure. This requires as many features as possible that transparently reroute traffic around MDF problems.

In addition to the raw Layer 3 performance discussed earlier, other routing features can be important in MDF situations. For example, the issue of what Layer 3 protocols the router handles can be important (IP, IPX, AppleTalk, and so forth). Routing protocol support (OSPF, RIP, EIGRP, IS-IS, and so on) can also be a factor. Support for features such as DHCP relay and HSRP can be critical.

Three types of devices can be utilized in MDF closets:

- Layer 2 switches
- Hybrid, "routing switches" such as MLS
- "Switching routers" such as the Catalyst 8500

The first of these is also the simplest—a Layer 2 switch. The moderate cost and high throughput of these devices can make them very attractive options. Examples of these devices include current Catalyst 4000 models and traditional Catalyst 5000 switches without a Route Switch Module (RSM) or NFFC.

However, as mentioned earlier, there are compelling reasons to use Layer 3 processing in the MDF. This leads many network designs to utilize the third option, a Layer 3 switch that is functioning as a hardware-based router, what Chapter 11 of *Cisco LAN Switching* referred to as a switching router. The Catalyst 8500 is an excellent example of this sort of device.

Cisco also offers another approach, Multilayer Switching (MLS), that lies between the previous two. MLS is a hybrid approach that allows the Layer 2-oriented Supervisors to cache Layer 3 information. It allows Catalysts to operate under the routing switch form of Layer 3 switching discussed in Chapter 11 of *Cisco LAN Switching*. A Catalyst 5000 with an RSM and NFFC is an example of an MLS switch. Other examples include the Catalyst 5000 Route Switch Feature Card (RSFC) and the Catalyst 6000 Multilayer Switch Feature Card (MSFC).

NOTE	It is important to understand the differences between the routing switch (MLS) and switching router (Catalyst 8500) styles of Layer 3 switching. These concepts are discussed in detail in Chapter 11 of *Cisco LAN Switching*.

Although the switching router (8500) and routing switch (MLS) options both offer very high throughput at Layer 3 and/or 4, there are important differences. For a thorough discussion of the technical differences, please see Chapter 11 of *Cisco LAN Switching*. This chapter and Chapter 15 of *Cisco LAN Switching* focus on the important design implications of these differences.

TIP	The most important MDF factors are availability and Layer 3 throughput and capabilities.

Three-Layer Campus Network Model: Access, Distribution, Core

The IDF/MDF terminology discussed in the previous section describes the world in terms of two layers. However, MDF interconnections can often be better described with a third layer. For this reason, it is often useful to describe campus (and WAN) networks in terms of a three-layer model that more accurately describes the unique requirements of the inter-MDF connections. Geoff Haviland's excellent Cisco Internetwork Design (CID) course has popularized the use of the terms access, distribution, and core to describe these three layers. Figure 2-3 illustrates the three-layer model.

Figure 2-3 *The Three-Layer Design Model*

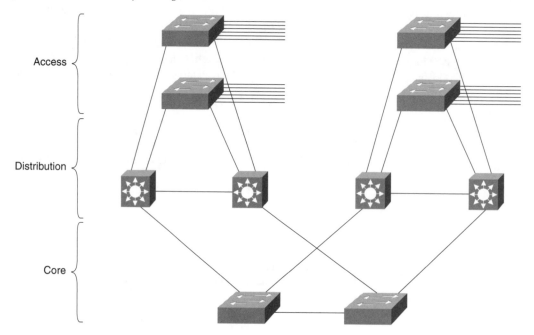

Each of these layers is briefly discussed in the following three sections.

Access Layer

The IDF closets are termed *access layer* closets under the three-layer model. The idea is that the devices deployed in these closets should be optimized for end-user access. Access layer requirements here are the same as those discussed in the IDF section: port density, cost, resiliency, and ease of management.

Distribution Layer

Under the three-layer model, MDF devices become *distribution layer* devices. The requirement for high Layer 3 throughput and functionality is especially important here.

TIP   In campus networks, the term *access layer* is synonymous with IDF, and *distribution layer* is equivalent to MDF.

Core Layer

The connections between the MDF switches become the *core layer* under the three-layer model. As is discussed in detail later, some networks have a very simple core consisting of several inter-MDF links or a pair of Layer 2 switches. In other cases, the size of the network might require Layer 3 switching within the core. Many networks utilize an Ethernet-based core; others might use ATM technology.

NOTE	In general, the terms *access layer* and *distribution layer* are used interchangeably with IDF and MDF. However, the IDF/MDF terms are used most often when discussing two-layer network designs; the access/distribution/core terminology is used when explaining three-layer topologies.

Key Requirements of Campus Designs

The "ideal" campus network should strive to achieve certain objectives. Some of these aspects have already been mentioned, but several new and important issues are introduced here (the new points are mentioned first):

- **Load balancing**—Given redundant paths, load balancing allows you to utilize all of the bandwidth you paid for. As is discussed in more detail in Chapter 15 of *Cisco LAN Switching*, flexibility, intelligence, and ease of configuration can be critical factors when utilizing this important feature.

- **Deterministic traffic patterns**—Traffic that flows in predictable ways can be crucial to network performance and troubleshooting. This can be especially true during network failure and recovery situations.

- **Consistent number of hops**—One of the principle factors contributing to deterministic traffic flows is a consistent number of hops throughout the network. As is discussed later in the chapter, this can best be achieved through a modular and consistent design.

- **Ease of configuration**—The network should not be excessively difficult to initially configure.

- **Ease of maintenance**—Ongoing maintenance tasks should be minimized. Where required, the tasks should follow well-established patterns that allow "cookie cutter" configurations.

- **Ease of troubleshooting**—Some designs can appear extremely appealing on paper, but they are a nightmare to troubleshoot (for example, extremely flat networks). A good design utilizes scalable modules or building blocks to promote easy troubleshooting through consistency and predictability.

- **Redundancy**—A 10–20 percent increase in hardware costs can increase network reliability by several hundred percent.

- **Cost**—Cost per port is especially important for high-density IDF devices.

Advantages of Routing

One of the key themes that is developed throughout this chapter is the idea that routing is critical to scalable network design. Hopefully, this is not news to you. However, given the recent popularity and focus on extremely flat, "avoid-the-router" designs, a fair amount of attention is devoted to this subject. Many people are convinced that the key objective in campus network design is to eliminate as many routers as possible. On the contrary, my experience suggests that this is exactly the wrong aim—routers have a proven track record of being the key to achieving the requirements of campus design discussed in the previous section.

- **Scalable bandwidth**—Routers have traditionally been considered slower than other approaches used for data forwarding. However, because a routed network uses a very decentralized algorithm, higher aggregate rates can be achieved than with less intelligent and more centralized Layer 2 forwarding schemes. Combine this fact with newer hardware-based routers (Layer 3 switches) and routing can offer extraordinary forwarding performance.

- **Broadcast filtering**—One of the Achilles heels of Layer 2 switching is broadcast containment. Vendors introduced VLANs as a partial solution to this problem, but key issues remain. Not only do broadcasts rob critical bandwidth resources, they also starve out CPU resources. Techniques such as ISL and LANE NICs that allow servers to connect to multiple VLANs in an attempt to build flat networks with a minimal use of routers only make this situation much worse—now the server must process the broadcasts for 10 or 20 VLANs! On the other hand, the more intelligent forwarding algorithms used by Layer 3 devices allow broadcasts to be contained while still maintaining full connectivity.

- **Superior multicast handling**—Although progress is being made to improve multicast support for Layer 2 devices through schemes such as IGMP Snooping, CGMP, and 802.1p (see Chapter 13, "Multicast and Broadcast Services") of *Cisco LAN Switching*, it is extremely unlikely that these efforts will ever provide the comprehensive set of features offered by Layer 3. By running Layer 3 multicast protocols such as PIM, routers always provide a vast improvement in multicast efficiency and scalability. Given the predictions for dramatic multicast growth, this performance will likely be critical to the future (or current) success of your network.

- **Optimal path selection**—Because of their sophisticated metrics and path determination algorithms, routing protocols offer much better path selection capabilities than Layer 2 switches. As discussed in the Spanning Tree chapters, Layer 2 devices can easily send traffic through many unnecessary bridge hops.

- **Fast convergence**—Not only do routing protocols pick optimal paths; they do it very quickly. Modern Layer 3 routing protocols generally converge in 5–10 seconds. On the other hand, Layer 2 Spanning-Tree Protocol (STP) convergence takes 30–50 seconds by default. Although it is possible to change the default STP timers and to make use of optimizations such as UplinkFast in certain topologies, it is very difficult to obtain the consistently speedy results offered by Layer 3 routing protocols.

- **Load balancing**—Routing protocols also have sophisticated load balancing mechanisms. Layer 3 load balancing is flexible, easy to configure, and supports many simultaneous paths. On the other hand, Layer 2 load balancing techniques such as the STP load balancing described in Chapter 7, "Advanced Spanning Tree," of *Cisco LAN Switching* can be extremely cumbersome and difficult to use.

- **Flexible path selection**—In addition to all of the other path selection benefits offered by routers, Cisco routers offer a wide variety of tools to manipulate path selections. Distribute lists, route maps, static routes, flexible metrics, and administrative distances are all examples of such mechanisms. These tools provide very granular control in a Layer 3 network.

- **Summarized addressing**—Layer 2 addresses use a flat address space. There is nothing about a MAC address that indicates physical location (it is much like a Social Security number). As a result, every bridging table in a flat network must contain an address for every node. On the other hand, Layer 3 addresses indicate location much like a ZIP code (postal code) or a telephone number's area code. By allowing addresses to be summarized, this hierarchical approach can allow *much* larger networks to be built. As a result, forwarding tables not only shrink dramatically in size, the address learning or routing table update process becomes much easier. Finally, lookups in the forwarding tables can be much faster.

- **Policy and access lists**—Most Layer 2 switches have very limited, if any, filtering capabilities. When filtering or access lists are supported, they use MAC addresses, hardly an efficient way to implement policy. On the other hand, routers can be used to provide complex access lists that function on Layer 3 and 4 information. This is much more useful from a policy implementation perspective. Hardware-based access lists are becoming increasingly common and flexible in Layer 3 switches.

- **Value-added features**—Although it is unlikely that the switching router Layer 3 devices such as the Catalyst 8500 will support "high touch" WAN-oriented services such as DLSw+ and protocol translation, there are still a large number of extremely important features that are offered by these platforms. For example, technologies such as DHCP relay, proxy ARP, debug, and proxy GNS can be critical router-based features in campus networks. (Note that some Layer 3 platforms can perform "high touch" services by running them in software. For example, MLS using an RSM could do DLSw+ on the RSM. The native IP traffic uses the NFFC for wire-speed forwarding; the DLSw+ is dependent on slower software-based forwarding.)

TIP Large networks almost always benefit from scalability, flexibility, and intelligence of routing. Try to build routing (Layer 3 switching) into your campus design.

Campus Design Models

Although a myriad of permutations and variations exist, most campus designs can be grouped into three categories:

- Traditional router and hub model
- Campus-wide VLANs model (also known as flat earth and end-to-end VLANs)
- Multilayer model

The sections that follow go into more detail on each of these campus design models.

Router and Hub Model

Figure 2-4 illustrates the traditional router and hub model.

Figure 2-4 *Router and Hub Model*

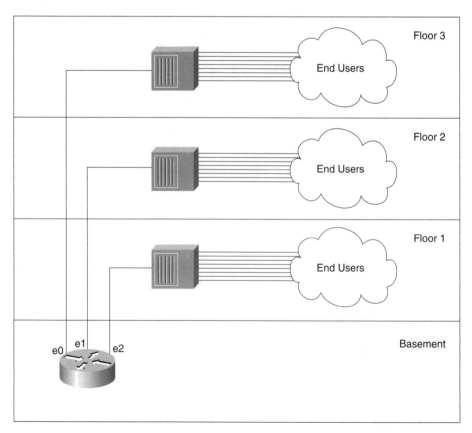

The traditional router and hub model uses Layer 1 hubs in IDF/access wiring closets. These connect back to unique ports on routers located in MDF/distribution closets. Several options are available for the campus core. In one approach, the distribution layer routers directly interconnect to form the network core/backbone. Because of its reliability and performance, an FDDI ring has traditionally been the media of choice for these connections. In other cases, some network designers prefer to form a collapsed backbone with a hub or router.

There are several advantages to the router and hub model as well as several reasons why most new designs have shied away from this approach. Table 2-1 lists the advantages and disadvantages of the router and hub model.

Table 2-1   *Advantages and Disadvantages of the Router and Hub Model*

Advantage	Disadvantage
Its reliance on routers makes for very good broadcast and multicast control.	Shared-media hubs do not offer enough bandwidth for modern applications. For example, in Figure 2-2, each floor must share a single 10 Megabit segment (factor in normal Ethernet overhead and these segments become extremely slow).
Because each hub represents a unique IP subnet or IPX network, administration is straightforward and easy to understand.	This design generally uses software-based routers that cannot keep up with increasing traffic levels.
Given moderate levels of traffic and departmental servers located on the local segment, the router and hub model can yield adequate performance.	Traffic patterns have changed, invalidating the assumption that most traffic would remain local. As a result, the campus-wide VLANs model became popular.
The hardware for this model is readily available and inexpensive.	

The chief advantage of this approach is the simplicity and familiarity that it brings to campus network design and management. The primary disadvantage is the limited bandwidth that this shared-media approach offers. The multilayer design model discussed later attempts to capitalize on the simplicity of the router and hub model while completely avoiding the limited bandwidth issue through the use of Layer 2 and 3 switching technology.

Campus-Wide VLANs Model

As people began to notice their router and hub networks struggling to keep up with traffic demands, they looked for alternate approaches. Many of these organizations decided to implement campus-wide VLANs, also known as the flat earth and end-to-end VLAN approach to network design.

Campus-wide VLANs strive to eliminate the use of routers. Because routers had become a significant bottleneck in campus networks, people looked for ways to minimize their use. Because broadcast domains still needed to be held to a reasonable size, VLANs were used to create logical barriers to broadcasts. Figure 2-5 illustrates a typical campus-wide VLANs design.

Figure 2-5   *Campus-Wide VLAN Model*

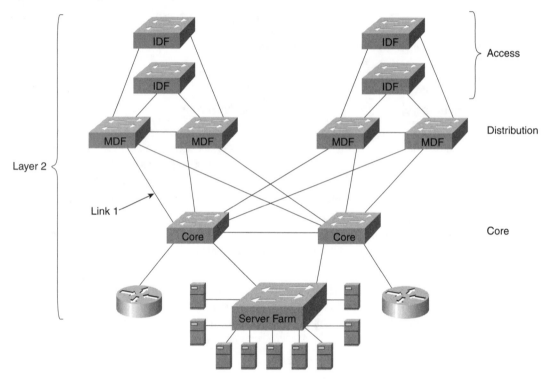

Figure 2-5 uses Layer 2 switching throughout the entire network. To provide communication between VLANs, two routers have been provided using the router-on-a-stick configuration (see Chapter 11 of *Cisco LAN Switching*).

Advantages of Campus-Wide VLANs

As the paragraphs that follow attest, there are some alluring aspects to the flat earth approach.

First, the campus-wide VLANs model allows network designers to create a direct Layer 2 path from end stations to the most commonly used servers. By deploying Layer 2 switching in all three layers of the access/distribution/core model, campus-wide VLANs should dramatically increase available bandwidth.

The second advantage of the campus-wide VLANs model is that VLANs can be used to provide logical control over broadcast domains and, therefore, subnets. Some platforms allow the switches to automatically detect what VLAN an end station should be assigned to, requiring no administration for adds, moves, and changes. Other schemes allow for more centralized control over VLAN assignments and strive to make the administration as easy as possible. For example, vendors can provide demos of glitzy products that allow you to drag-and-drop end users into VLANs. Other examples include Cisco's Virtual Management Policy Server (VMPS) that makes VLAN assignments based on MAC addresses and User Registration Tool (URT) that uses NT directory services (VMPS and URT are discussed in the section "VMPS and Dynamic VLANs: Advanced Administration" of Chapter 5, "VLANs" in *Cisco LAN Switching*).

The third advantage of campus-wide VLANs is that traffic only goes through a router if it needs to cross VLAN boundaries. If a user in the Finance VLAN needs to access the Finance server (located in the same VLAN), no routers are involved. However, if this user needs to occasionally access a server in the Marketing VLAN, a router is used. Servers can even be directly connected to multiple VLANs through the use of ISL or LANE NICs, further reducing the requirement for routers. For example, the server in the Marketing VLAN can be fitted with an ISL NIC to allow direct, Layer 2 access from the Finance VLAN.

Finally, this centralized use of routing can make it much easier to configure access lists and security in the network. For example, consider the case of a college network where two VLANs exist: students and professors. These two VLANs might span dozens of buildings, but because of the centralized routing typically used with campus-wide VLANs, access lists might only need to be configured on a pair of routers. On the other hand, if every building on campus connected to the campus backbone through a router, the network might require hundreds of access lists scattered across many dozens of routers.

The end result: you have the speed of Layer 2, the flexibility of VLANs, and you have avoided the "slowness" of the router.

Disadvantages of Campus-Wide VLANs

There are also some significant downsides to the campus-wide VLANs model:

- Management difficulties
- Lack of logical structure
- Large and overlapping Spanning Tree domains
- It is easy for a problem in one VLAN to deplete bandwidth in all VLANs across trunk links
- Many networks using campus-wide VLANs must resort to eliminating all redundancy to achieve network stability
- Lack of scalability

- Most modern traffic violates the "stay in one subnet" rule employed by the campus-wide VLAN model
- Modern routers are not a bottleneck

The paragraphs that follow provide more detailed coverage of each of these disadvantages.

Management of these networks can be much more difficult and tedious than originally expected. The router and hub design had the logical clarity of one subnet per wiring closet. Conversely, many networks using campus-wide VLANs have developed into a confusing mess of VLAN and Layer 3 address assignments.

Another downside to campus-wide VLANs is that the lack of logical structure can be problematic, especially when it comes to troubleshooting. Without a clearly defined hierarchy, it is very difficult to narrow down the source of each problem. Before each troubleshooting session, valuable time can be wasted trying to understand the constantly changing VLAN structure.

Also, campus-wide VLANs result in large and overlapping Spanning Tree domains. As discussed in Chapter 6, "Understanding Spanning Tree," and Chapter 7, "Advanced Spanning Tree," of *Cisco LAN Switching*, STP uses a complex set of evaluations that elect one central device (the Root Bridge) for every VLAN. Other bridges and switches then locate the shortest path to this central bridge/switch and use this path for all data forwarding. The Spanning-Tree Protocol is extremely dynamic—if the Root Bridge (or a link to the Root Bridge) is "flapping," the network continuously vacillates between the two switches acting as the Root Bridge (disrupting traffic every time it does so). Large Spanning Tree domains must use very conservative timer values, resulting in frustratingly slow failover performance. Also, as the size and number of the Spanning Tree domains grow, the possibility of CPU overload increases. If a single device in a single VLAN falls behind and opens up a loop, this can quickly overload every device connected to every VLAN. The result: network outages that last for days and are difficult to troubleshoot.

Yet another downside to campus-wide VLANs is that the wide use of trunk links that carry multiple VLANs makes the Spanning Tree problems even worse. For example, consider Link 1 in Figure 2-5, a Fast Ethernet link carrying VLANs 1–15. Assume that the CPU in a single switch in VLAN 1 becomes overloaded and opens up a bridging loop. Although the loop might be limited to VLAN 1, this VLAN's traffic can consume all of the trunk's capacity and starve out all other VLANs. This problem is even worse if you further assume that VLAN 1 is the management VLAN. In this case, the broadcasts caught in the bridging loop devour 100 percent of switch's CPU horsepower throughout the network. As more and more switch CPUs become overloaded, more and more VLANs experience bridging loops. Within a matter of seconds, the entire network "melts down."

An additional problem with the campus-wide VLAN model is that, to avoid these Spanning Tree and trunking problems, many campus-wide VLAN networks have had to resort to eliminating all redundant paths just to achieve stability. To solve this problem, redundant links can be physically disconnected or trunks can be pruned in such a way that a loop-free Spanning Tree is manually created. In either case, this makes every device in the network a single point of failure. Most network designers never intend to make this sort of sacrifice when they sign up for a flat earth design. Without routers, there are no Layer 3 "barriers" in the network and it becomes very easy for problems to spread throughout the entire campus.

Furthermore, campus-wide VLANs are not scalable. Many small networks have been successfully deployed using the campus-wide VLAN design. Initially, the users of these networks are usually very happy with both the utility and the bandwidth of their new infrastructure. However, as the network begins to grow in size, the previously mentioned problems become more and more chronic.

Yet another downside to campus-wide VLANs is that it is harder and harder to bypass routers, the very premise that the entire campus-wide VLANs scheme was built upon. As traffic patterns have evolved from departmental servers on the local segment to enterprise servers located in a centralized server farm, it has become very difficult to remove routers from this geographically dispersed path. For example, it can be difficult to connect an enterprise web server to 20 or more VLANs (subnets) without going through a router. A variety of solutions such as ISL, 802.1Q, and LANE NICs have become available; however, these have generally produced very disappointing performance. And, as mentioned earlier, these NICs request the server to process all broadcasts for all VLANs, robbing it of valuable and expensive CPU cycles. Also, the multiple-VLAN NICs have been fraught with other problems such as slow initialization time, a limited number of VLANs, and unexpected server behavior.

Finally, another basic premise of the campus-wide VLAN strategy is no longer true. Specifically, routers are now as fast (or nearly as fast) as Layer 2 switches. Although this equivalent performance generally comes at a price premium, it is no longer worthwhile to go to such great lengths to avoid Layer 3 routing.

Practical Advice Regarding Campus-Wide VLANs

I have implemented several networks utilizing the campus-wide VLAN approach. Prior to 1998, routers were simply too slow to place them in the middle of burgeoning campus traffic levels. Although I often had this nagging feeling about the lack of Layer 3 hierarchy, I jumped on the bandwagon with everyone else. In short, there simply didn't seem to be another option. However, with the advent of Layer 3 switching, I see fewer and fewer compelling uses for campus-wide VLANs.

Before leaving you with the feeling that everyone using campus-wide VLANs hates it, I should also point out that there are some fairly large networks utilizing this model with great success. Whether it is because their traffic patterns still adhere to the 80/20 rule or they like to take advantage of the drag-and-drop approach to VLANs, some network administrators firmly support this style of network design.

However, I have talked to far more clients that have struggled to produce stable and scalable networks using this model. For many users, the disadvantages discussed earlier are far too debilitating to justify the advantages of the campus-wide VLAN design.

Carefully evaluate the downsides of the campus-wide model before designing your network in this manner. Although some users are very happy with this approach to campus design, most have been disappointed with the stability and scalability.

Multilayer Model

The multilayer model strives to provide the stability and scalability of the router and hub model while also capturing the performance of the campus-wide VLANs model. This approach takes full advantage of hardware-based routing, Layer 3 switching, to put routing back into its rightful place. However, it does not ignore Layer 2 switching. In fact, it seeks to strike the optimal balance—Layer 3 switching is used for control, whereas Layer 2 switching is used for cost-effective data forwarding.

Figure 2-6 illustrates a sample network using the multilayer model.

Figure 2-6   *Multilayer Model*

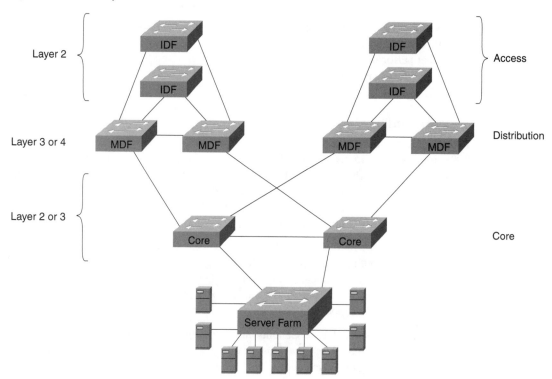

Each IDF/MDF cluster forms a separate module in the design. Figure 2-6 shows two modules. The access layer IDF switches use Layer 2 forwarding to provide large amounts of cost-effective bandwidth. The distribution layer MDF switches provide the Layer 3 control that is required in all large networks. These IDF/MDF modules then connect through a variety of Layer 2 or Layer 3 cores.

TIP   The multilayer model combines Layer 2 and Layer 3 processing into a cohesive whole. This design has proven to be highly flexible and scalable.

In general, the multilayer model is the recommended approach for enterprise campus design for several reasons.

First, the use of routers provides adequate Layer 3 control. In short, this allows all of the benefits discussed in the "Advantages of Routing" section to accrue to your network. Without listing all of these advantages again, a multilayer design is scalable, flexible, high performance, and easy to manage.

Second, as its name suggests, the multilayer model offers hierarchy. In hierarchical networks, layers with specific roles are defined to allow large and consistent designs. As the next section discusses, this allows each layer of the access/distribution/core model to meet unique and specific requirements.

Third, this approach is very modular. There are many benefits to a modular design, including the following:

- It is easy to grow the network.
- The total available bandwidth scales as additional modules are added.
- Modular networks are easier to understand, troubleshoot, and maintain.
- The network can use cookie cutter configurations. This consistency saves administrative headaches while also reducing the chance of configuration errors.
- It is easier to migrate to a modular network. The old network can appear as another module (although it does not have the consistent layout and configurations of modules in the new network).
- Modular networks allow consistent and deterministic traffic patterns.
- Modular designs promote load balancing and redundancy.
- It is much easier to provide fast failover in a consistent, modular design than it is in less structured designs. Because the topology is constrained and well defined, both Layer 2 and Layer 3 convergence benefit.
- Modular networks allow technologies to be easily substituted for one another. Not only does this allow organizations more freedom in the initial design (for example, the core can be either Ethernet or ATM), it makes it easier to upgrade the network in the long run.

General Recommendation: Multilayer Model

As discussed in the previous section, the multilayer model is the most appropriate approach for most modern campus networks for a variety of reasons. This section explains some specific considerations of this model.

Distribution Blocks

A large part of the benefit of the multilayer model centers around the concept of a modular approach to access (IDF) and distribution (MDF) switches. Given a pair of redundant MDF switches, each IDF/access layer switch forms a triangle of connectivity as shown in Figure 2-7. If there are ten IDF switches connected to a given set of MDF switches, ten triangles are formed (such as might be the case in a ten-story building). The collection of all triangles formed by two MDF switches is referred to as a *distribution block*. Most commonly, a distribution block equates to all of the IDF and MDF switches located in a single building.

Figure 2-7   *Triangles of Connectivity within a Distribution Block*

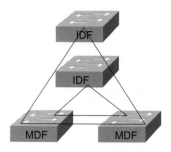

Because of its simplicity, the triangle creates the ideal building block for a campus network. By having two vertical links (IDF uplink connections), it automatically provides redundancy. Because the redundancy is formed in a predictable, consistent, and uncomplicated fashion, it is much easier to provide uniformly fast failover performance.

TIP   Use the concept of a distribution block to simplify the design and maintenance of your network.

The multilayer model does not take a dogmatic stance on Layer 2 versus Layer 3 switching (although it is based around the theme that *some* Layer 3 processing is a requirement in large networks). Instead, it seeks to create the optimal blend of both Layer 2 and Layer 3 technology to achieve the competing goals of low cost, high performance, and scalability.

To provide cost-effective bandwidth, Layer 2 switches are generally used in the IDF (access layer) wiring closets. As discussed earlier, the NetFlow Feature Card can add significant value in the wiring closet with features such as Protocol Filtering and IGMP Snooping.

To provide control, Layer 3 switching should be deployed in the MDF (distribution layer) closets. This is probably the single-most important aspect of the entire design. Without the Layer 3 component, the distribution blocks are no longer self-contained units. A lack of Layer 3 processing in the distribution layer causes Spanning Tree, VLANs, and broadcast domains to spread throughout the entire network. This increases the interdependency of various pieces of the network, making the network far less scalable and far more likely to suffer a network-wide outage.

By making use of Layer 3 switching, each distribution block becomes an independent switching system. The benefits discussed in the "Advantages of Routing" section are baked into the network. Problems that develop in one part of the network are prevented from spreading to other parts of the network.

You should also be careful to not circumvent the modularity of the distribution block concept with random links. For example, Links 1 and 2 in Figure 2-8 break the modularity of the multilayer model.

Figure 2-8   *Links 1 and 2 Break the Modularity of the Multilayer Design*

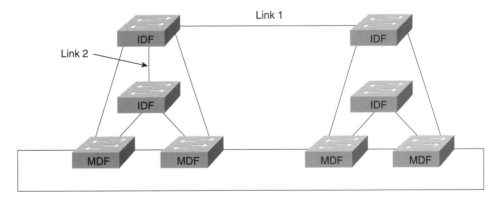

The intent here was good: provide a direct, Layer 2 path between three IDF switches containing users in the same workgroup. Although this does eliminate one or two router hops from the paths between these IDF switches, it causes the entire design to start falling apart. Soon another exception is made, then another, and so on. Before long, the entire network begins to resemble an interconnected mess more like a bowl of spaghetti than a carefully planned campus network. Just remember that the scalability and long-term health of the network are more important than a short-term boost in bandwidth. Avoid "spaghetti networks" at all costs.

TIP Be certain to maintain the modularity of distribution blocks. Do not add links or inter-VLAN bridging that violate the Layer 3 barrier that the multilayer model uses in the distribution layer.

Without descending too far into "marketing speak," it is useful to note the potential application of Layer 4 switching in the distribution layer. By considering transport layer port numbers in addition to network layer addressing, Layer 4 switching can more easily facilitate policy-based networking. However, from a scalability and performance standpoint, Layer 4 switching does not have a major impact on the overall multilayer model—it still creates the all-important Layer 3 barrier at the MDF switches.

On the other hand, the choice of Layer 3 switching technology can make a difference in matters such as addressing and load balancing.

Switching Router (8500) MDFs

In the case of 8500-style switching routers, the MDF switches make a complete break in the Layer 2 topology by default. As a result, the triangles of connectivity appear as two unique subnets—one that crosses the IDF switch and one that sits between the MDF switches as illustrated in Figure 2-9.

Figure 2-9 *Switching Router MDF Switches Break the Network into Two Subnets*

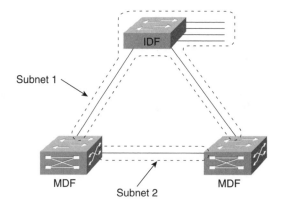

The resulting network is completely free of Layer 2 loops. Although some network designers have viewed this as an opportunity to completely disable the Spanning-Tree Protocol, this is generally not advisable because misconfiguration errors can easily create loops in the IDF wiring closet or end-user work areas (therefore possibly taking down the entire IDF). However, it does mean that STP load balancing cannot be used. Recall from Chapter 7 of *Cisco LAN Switching* that STP load balancing requires two characteristics to be present in the network. First, it requires redundant paths, something that exists in Figure 2-9. Second, it requires that these redundant paths form Layer 2 loops, something that the routers in Figure 2-9 prevent. Therefore, some other load balancing technique must be employed.

NOTE	The decision of whether or not the Spanning-Tree Protocol should be disabled can be complex. This book recommends leaving Spanning Tree enabled (even in Layer 2 loop-free networks such as the one in Figure 2-9) because it provides a safety net for any loops that might be accidentally formed through the end-user ports. Currently, most organizations building large-scale campus networks want to take this conservative stance. This choice seems especially wise when you consider that Spanning Tree does not impose any failover delay for important topology changes such as a broken IDF uplink. In other words, the use of Spanning Tree in this environment provides an important benefit while having very few downsides. For more discussion on the technical intricacies of the Spanning-Tree Protocol, see Chapters 6 and 7 of *Cisco LAN Switching*. For more detailed and specific recommendations on using the Spanning-Tree Protocol in networks utilizing the various forms of Layer 3 switching, see Chapter 15 of *Cisco LAN Switching*.

In general, some form of HSRP load balancing is the most effective solution. As discussed in the "HSRP" section of Chapter 11 of *Cisco LAN Switching*, if the IDF switch contains multiple end-user VLANs, the VLANs can be configured to alternate active HSRP peers between the MDF switches. For example, the left switch in Figure 2-9 could be configured as the active HSRP peer for the odd VLANs, whereas the right switch would handle the even VLANs. However, if the network only contains a single VLAN on the IDF switch (this is often done to simplify network administration by making it more like the router and hub model), the Multigroup HSRP (MHSRP) technique is usually the most appropriate technology. Figure 2-10 illustrates the MHSRP approach.

Figure 2-10 *MHSRP Load Balancing*

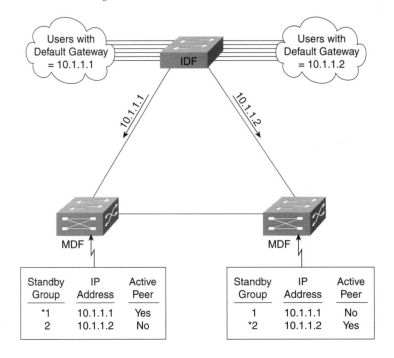

Standby Group	IP Address	Active Peer
*1	10.1.1.1	Yes
2	10.1.1.2	No

Standby Group	IP Address	Active Peer
1	10.1.1.1	No
*2	10.1.1.2	Yes

In Figure 2-10, two HSRP groups are created for a single subnet/VLAN. The first group uses the address **10.1.1.1**, whereas the second group uses **10.1.1.2**. Notice that both addresses intentionally fall within the same subnet. Half of the end stations connected to the IDF switch are then configured to use a primary default gateway of **10.1.1.1**, and the other half use **10.1.1.2** (this can be automated with DHCP). For more information on this technique, see the "MHSRP" section of Chapter 11 of *Cisco LAN Switching* and the "Use DHCP to Solve User Mobility Problems" section of Chapter 15 in *Cisco LAN Switching*.

TIP

In general, implementing load balancing while using switching routers in the distribution layer requires multiple IDF VLANs (each with a separate HSRP standby group) or MHSRP for a single IDF VLAN.

Routing Services (MLS) MDFs

However, if the MDF switches are using routing switch MLS-style Layer 3 switching, the design might be very different. In this case, it is entirely possible to have Layer 2 loops. Rather than being pure routers as with the switching router approach, the MDF switches are normal Layer 2 devices that have been enhanced with Layer 3 caching technology. Therefore, MLS devices pass Layer 2 traffic by default (this default can be changed). For example, Figure 2-11 illustrates the Layer 2 loops that commonly result when MLS is in use.

Figure 2-11   *MLS Often Creates Layer 2 Loops that Require STP Load Balancing*

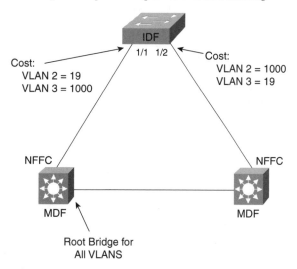

Both VLANs 2 and 3 are assigned to all three trunk links, forming a Layer 2 loop. In this case, STP load balancing is required. As shown in Figure 2-11, the cost for VLAN 3 on the 1/1 IDF port can be increased to 1000, and the same can be done for VLAN 2 on Port 1/2. For more detailed information on STP load balancing, please see Chapter 7 of *Cisco LAN Switching*.

TIP   The Layer 2/3 hybrid nature of MLS generally requires STP load balancing.

Core

Designing the core of a multilayer network is one of the areas where creativity and careful planning can come into play. Unlike the distribution blocks, there is no set design for a multilayer core. This section discusses some of the design factors that should be taken into consideration.

One of the primary concerns when designing a campus core backbone should be fast failover and convergence behavior. Because of the reliance on Layer 3 processing in the MLS design, fast-converging routing protocols can be used instead of the slower Spanning-Tree Protocol. However, one must be careful to avoid unexpected Spanning Tree slowdowns within the core itself.

Another concern is that of VLANs. In some cases, the core can utilize a single flat VLAN that spans one or more Layer 2 core switches. In other cases, traffic can be segregated into

VLANs for a variety of reasons. For example, multiple VLANs can be used for policy reasons or to separate the different Layer 3 protocols. A separate management VLAN is also desirable when using Layer 2-oriented switches.

Broadcast and multicast traffic are other areas of concern. As much as possible, broadcasts should be kept off of the network's core. Because the multilayer model uses Layer 3 switching in the MDF devices, this usually isn't an issue. Likewise, multicast traffic also benefits from the use of routers in the multilayer model. If the core makes use of routing, Protocol Independent Multicast (PIM) can be used to dynamically build optimized multicast distribution trees. If sparse-mode PIM is used, the rendezvous point (RP) can be placed on a Layer 3 switch in the core. If the core is comprised of Layer 2 switches only, then CGMP or IGMP Snooping can be deployed to reduce multicast flooding within the core.

One of the important decisions facing every campus network designer has to do with the choice of media and switching technology. The majority of campus networks currently utilize Fast and Gigabit Ethernet within the core. However, ATM can be a viable choice in many cases. Because it supports a wide range of services, can integrate well with wide area networks, and provides extremely low-latency switching, ATM has many appealing aspects. Also, MultiProtocol Label Swapping (MPLS, also known as Tag Switching), traditionally seen as a WAN-only technology, is likely to become increasingly common in very large campus backbones. Because it provides excellent traffic engineering capabilities and very tight integration between Layer 2 and 3, MPLS can be extremely useful in all sorts of network designs.

However, the most critical decision has to do with the switching characteristics of the core. In some cases, a Layer 2 core is optimal; other networks benefit from a Layer 3 core. The following sections discuss issues particular to each.

Layer 2 Core

Figure 2-12 depicts the typical Layer 2 core in a multilayer network.

Figure 2-12   *A Layer 2 Core*

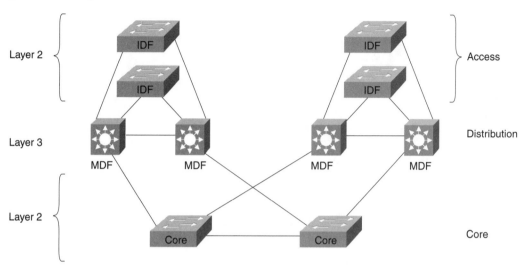

This creates a L2/L3/L2 profile throughout the network. The network's intelligence is contained in the distribution-layer MDF switches. Both the access (IDF) and core switches utilize Layer 2 switching to maintain a high price/performance ratio. To provide redundancy, a pair of switches form the core. Because the core uses Layer 2 processing, this approach is most suitable for small to medium campus backbones.

When building a Layer 2 core, Spanning Tree failover performance should be closely analyzed. Otherwise, the entire network can suffer from excessively slow reconvergence. Because the equipment comprising the campus core should be housed in tightly controlled locations, it is often desirable to disable Spanning Tree entirely within the core of the network.

TIP

I recommend that you only disable Spanning Tree in the core if you are using switching routers in the distribution layer. If MLS is in use, its Layer 2 orientation makes it too easy to misconfigure a distribution switch and create a bridging loop.

One way to accomplish this is through the use of multiple VLANs that have been carefully assigned to links in a manner that create a loop-free topology within each VLAN. An alternate approach consists of physically removing cables that create Layer 2 loops. For example, consider Figure 2-13.

Figure 2-13 *A Loop-Free Core*

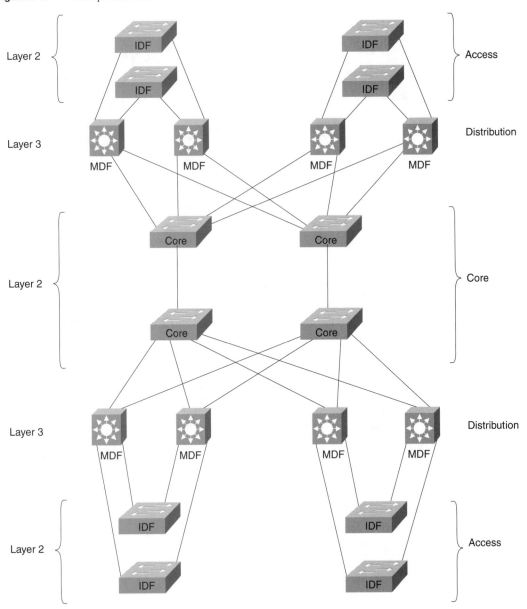

In Figure 2-13, the four Layer 2 switches forming the core have been kept loop free at Layer 2. Although a redundant path does exist through each distribution (MDF) switch, the pure routing behavior of these nodes prevents any Layer 2 loops from forming.

If Spanning Tree is required within the core, blocked ports should be closely analyzed. Because STP load balancing can be very tricky to implement in the network core, compromises might be necessary.

In addition to Spanning Tree, there are several other issues to look for in a Layer 2 core. First, be careful that multicast flooding is not a problem. As mentioned earlier, IGMP Snooping and CGMP can be useful tools in this situation (also see Chapter 13 of *Cisco LAN Switching*). Second, keep an eye on router peering limits as the network grows. Because each MDF switch is a router under the multilayer model, a Layer 2 core creates the appearance of many routers sitting around a single subnet. If the number of routers becomes too large, this can easily lead to excessive state information, erratic behavior, and slow convergence. In this case, it can be desirable to break the network into multiple VLANs that reduce peering.

TIP   Be careful to avoid excessive router peering when using Catalyst 8500s. One of the easiest ways to accomplish this is through the use of a Layer 3 core (see the next section).

A Layer 2 core can provide a very useful campus backbone. However, because of the potential issues and scaling limits, it is most appropriate in small to medium campus networks.

TIP   A Layer 2 core can be a cost-effective solution for smaller campus networks.

Layer 3 Core

Figure 2-14 redraws Figure 2-12 with a Layer 3 core.

Figure 2-14 *A Layer 3 Core*

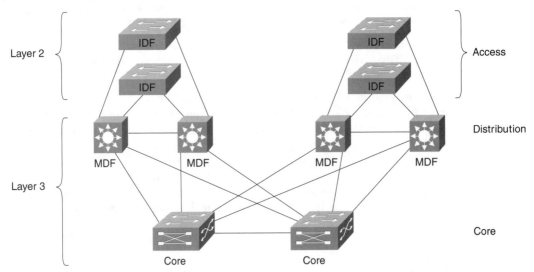

Although Figure 2-12 and Figure 2-14 look very similar, the use of Layer 3 switching within the core makes several important changes to the network.

First, the path determination is no longer contained only within the distribution layer switches. With a Layer 3 core, the path determination is spread throughout the distribution and core layer switches. This more decentralized approach can provide many benefits:

- Higher aggregate forwarding capacity
- Superior multicast control
- Flexible and easy to configure load balancing
- Scalability
- Router peering is reduced
- IOS feature throughout a large percentage of the network

In short, the power and flexibility of Layer 3 processing eliminates many of the issues discussed concerning Layer 2 backbones. For example, the switches can be connected in a wide variety of looped configurations without concern for bridging loops or STP performance. By cross-linking core switches, redundancy *and* performance can be maximized. Also, placing routing nodes within campus core, router mesh and peering between the distribution switches can be dramatically reduced (however, it is still advisable to consider areas of excessive router peering).

Notice that a Layer 3 core does add additional hops to the path of most traffic. In the case of a Layer 2 core, most traffic requires two hops, one through the end user's MDF switch and the other through the server farm's MDF switch. In the case of a Layer 3 core, an additional hop (or two) is added. However, several factors minimize this concern:

- The consistent and modular design of the multilayer model guarantees a consistent and small number of router hops. In general, no more than four router hops within the campus should ever be necessary.

- Many Layer 3 switches have latencies comparable to Layer 2 switches.

- Windowing protocols (such as TCP or IPX Burst Mode) reduce impact of latency for most applications.

- Switching latency is often a very small part of overall latency. In other words, latency is not as big an issue as most people make it out to be.

- The scalability benefits of Layer 3 are generally far more important than any latency concerns.

TIP   Larger campus networks benefit from a Layer 3 core.

Server Farm Design

Server farm design is an important part of almost all modern networks. The multilayer model easily accommodates this requirement. First, the server farm can easily be treated as its own distribution block. A pair of redundant Layer 3 switches can be used to provide physical redundancy as well as network layer redundancy with protocols such as HSRP. In addition, the Layer 3 switches create an ideal place to apply server-related policy and access lists. Figure 2-15 illustrates a server farm distribution block.

Figure 2-15 *The Server Farm Can Form Another Distribution Block*

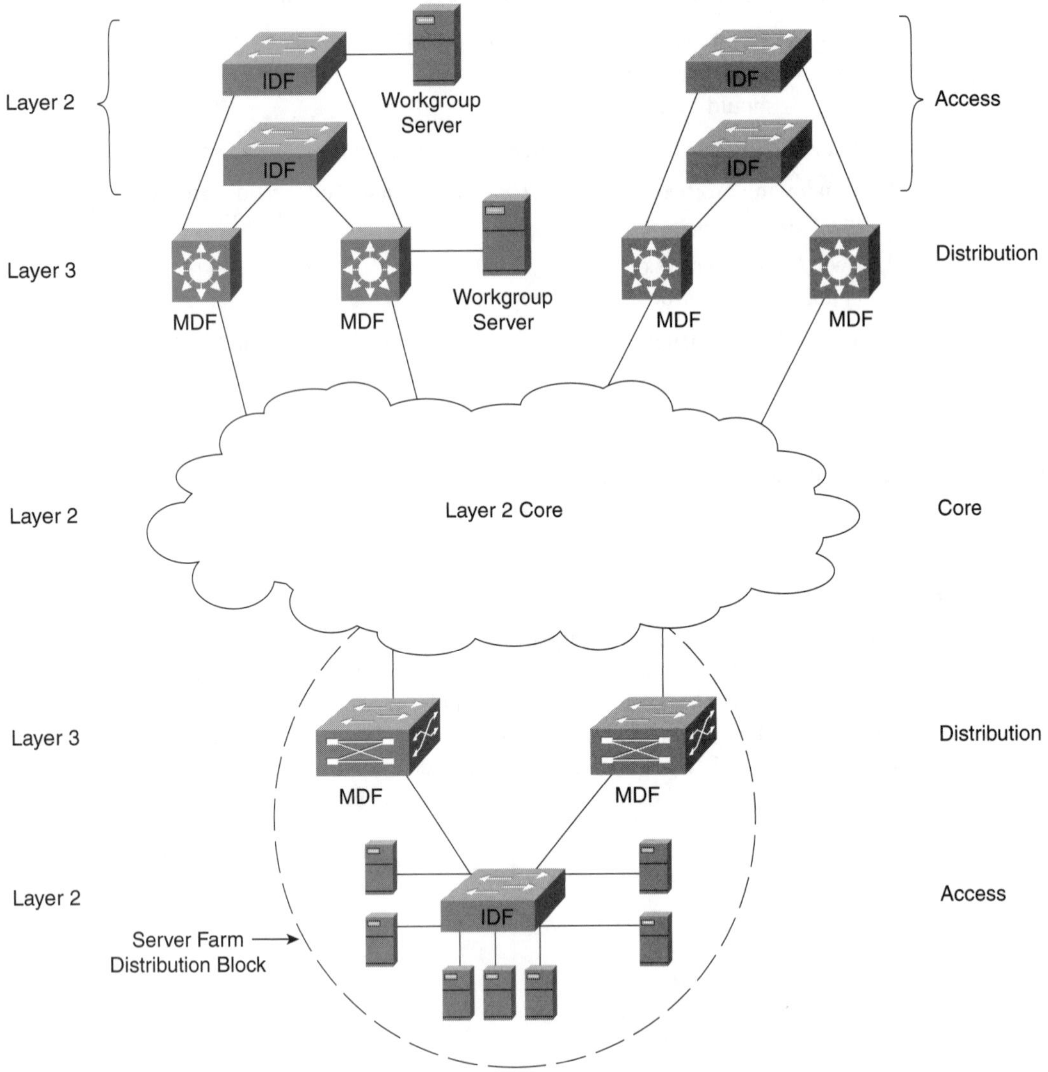

Although enterprise-wide servers should generally be deployed in a central location, workgroup servers can be attached directly to access or distribution level switches. Two examples of this are shown in Figure 2-15.

TIP An enterprise server farm is usually best implemented as another distribution block that connects to the core.

Specific tips for server farm design are discussed in considerably more detail in the "Server Farms" section of Chapter 15 in *Cisco LAN Switching*.

Using a Unique VTP Domain for Each Distribution Block

When using the MLS approach to Layer 3 switching in the MDF closets, it might be advantageous to make each distribution block a separate VTP domain. Because of the Layer 2 orientation to MLS, VLANs propagate throughout the entire network by default (see Chapter 12 of *Cisco LAN Switching* for more information on VTP). However, the multilayer model is designed to constrain VLANs to an individual distribution block. By innocently using the default behavior, your network can become unnecessarily burdened by extraneous VLANs and STP computations.

Assigning a unique VTP domain name to each distribution block is a simple but effective way to have VLAN propagation mirror the intended design. When a new VLAN is added within a distribution block, it automatically is added to every other switch in that block. However, because other distribution blocks are using a different domain name, they do not learn about this new VLAN.

TIP	The MLS approach to Layer 3 switching can lead to excessive VLAN propagation. Use a different VTP domain name for each distribution block to overcome this default behavior.

When VTP domains are in use, it is usually best to make the names descriptive of the distribution block (for example, Building1 and Building 2).

TIP	Recall from Chapter 8 of *Cisco LAN Switching* that when using trunk links between different VTP domains, the trunk state will need to be hard-coded to **on**. The use of **auto** and **desirable** will not work across VTP domain names (in other words, the DISL and DTP protocols check for matching VTP domain names).

IP Addressing

In a very large campus network, it is usually best to assign bitwise contiguous blocks of address spaces to each distribution block. This allows the routers in each distribution block to summarize all of the subnets within that block into a single advertisement that gets sent into the core backbone. For example, the single advertisement **10.1.16.0/20** (**/20** is a shorthand way to represent the subnet mask **255.255.240.0**) can summarize the entire range of 16 subnets from **10.1.16.0/24** to **10.1.31.0/24** (**/24** is equivalent to the subnet mask **255.255.255.0**). This is illustrated in Figure 2-16.

Figure 2-16 *Using IP Address Summarization*

128 64 32 16	8 4 2 1	128 64 32 16	8 4 2 1	128 64 32 16	8 4 2 1	128 64 32 16	8 4 2 1	
XXXX	XXXX	XXXX	XXXX	XXXX	XXXX	XXXX	XXXX	
Summary Address					← /20 Subnet Mask			
0000	1010	0000	0001	0001	0000	0000	0000	10.1.16.0/20
Summarized Addresses						← /24 Subnet Mask		
0000	1010	0000	0001	0001	0000	0000	0000	10.1.16.0/24
0000	1010	0000	0001	0001	0001	0000	0000	10.1.17.0/24
0000	1010	0000	0001	0001	0010	0000	0000	10.1.18.0/24
0000	1010	0000	0001	0001	0011	0000	0000	10.1.19.0/24
0000	1010	0000	0001	0001	0100	0000	0000	10.1.20.0/24
0000	1010	0000	0001	0001	0101	0000	0000	10.1.21.0/24
0000	1010	0000	0001	0001	0110	0000	0000	10.1.22.0/24
0000	1010	0000	0001	0001	0111	0000	0000	10.1.23.0/24
0000	1010	0000	0001	0001	1000	0000	0000	10.1.24.0/24
0000	1010	0000	0001	0001	1001	0000	0000	10.1.25.0/24
0000	1010	0000	0001	0001	1010	0000	0000	10.1.26.0/24
0000	1010	0000	0001	0001	1011	0000	0000	10.1.27.0/24
0000	1010	0000	0001	0001	1100	0000	0000	10.1.28.0/24
0000	1010	0000	0001	0001	1101	0000	0000	10.1.29.0/24
0000	1010	0000	0001	0001	1110	0000	0000	10.1.30.0/24
0000	1010	0000	0001	0001	1111	0000	0000	10.1.31.0/24

These 16 Entries Can Be Summarized into the Single /20 Above

First 20 Bits of All Addresses Match

As shown in Figure 2-16, the **/20** and **/24** subnet masks (or network prefixes) differ by four bits (in other words, **/20** is four bits "shorter" than **/24**). These are the only four bits that differ between the 16 **/24** subnet addresses. In other words, because all 16 **/24** subnet addresses match in the first 20 bits, a single **/20** address can be used to summarize all of them.

In a real-world distribution block, the 16 individual **/24** subnets can be applied to 16 different end-user VLANs. However, outside the distribution block, a classless IP routing protocol can distribute the single **/20** route of **10.1.16.0/20**.

TIP In very large campus networks, try to plan for future growth and address summarization by pre-allocating bitwise contiguous blocks of address space.

Scaling Link Bandwidth

Note that the modular nature of the multilayer model allows individual links to easily scale to higher bandwidth. Not only does the architecture accommodate entirely different media types, it is easy to add additional links and utilize Fast or Gigabit EtherChannel.

Network Migrations

Finally, the modularity of the multilayer model can make migrations much easier. In general, the entire old network can appear as a single distribution block to the rest of the new network (for example, imagine that the server farm distribution block in Figure 2-15 is the old network). Although the old network generally does not have all of the benefits of the multilayer model, it provides a redundant and routed linkage between the two networks. After the migration is complete, the old network can be disabled.

Exercises

This section includes a variety of questions on the topic of this chapter—campus design concepts and models. By completing these, you can test your mastery of the material included in this chapter as well as help prepare yourself for the CCIE written and lab tests.

Review Questions

1　What are some of the unique requirements of an IDF switch?

2　What are some of the unique requirements of an MDF switch?

3　Describe the access/distribution/core terminology.

4　Why is routing an important part of any large network design?

5　What networks work best with the router and hub model?

6　What are the benefits of the campus-wide VLANs model?

7　What are the downsides of the campus-wide VLANs model?

8　Describe the concept of a distribution block.

9　Why is it important to have modularity in a network?

10　What are the concerns that arise when using a Layer 2 core versus a Layer 3 core?

11　How should a server farm be implemented in the multilayer model?

Design Lab

Design two campus networks that meet the following requirements. The first design should employ the campus-wide VLANs model using Catalyst 5509 switches. The second design should implement the multilayer model by using Catalyst 8540 MDF switches and Catalyst 5509 IDF switches. Here are the requirements:

- The campus contains three buildings.
- Each building has four floors.

- Each floor has one IDF switch. (In reality there would be more, however, these can be eliminated from this exercise for simplicity.)

- Each building has two MDF switches in the basement.

- Each IDF has redundant links (one two each MDF switch).

- The MDF switches are fully or partially meshed (choose which one you feel is more appropriate) with Gigabit Ethernet links (in other words, the core does not use a third layer of switches).

- Each IDF switch should have a unique management VLAN where SC0 can be assigned.

- In the campus-wide VLANs design, assume there are 12 VLANs and that every IDF switch participates in every VLAN.

- In the multilayer design, assume that every IDF switch only participates in a single end-user VLAN (for administrative simplicity).

How many VLANs are required under both designs?

This chapter covers the following key topics:

- **VLANs**—The chapter begins with a range of virtual LAN (VLAN)-related topics from using VLANs to create a scalable design to pruning VLANs from trunk links.

- **Spanning Tree**—Covers important Spanning Tree issues that are essential to constructing a stable network.

- **Load Balancing**—Discusses the five techniques available for increasing campus network bandwidth.

- **Routing/Layer 3 Switching**—Discusses issues such as MLS (routing switches) and switching routers.

- **ATM**—Examines valid reasons for using ATM in your campus network and how to deploy it in a scalable fashion.

- **Campus Migrations**—Provides recommendations for migrating your campus network.

- **Server Farms**—Covers some basic server farm design principles.

- **Additional Campus Design Recommendations**—Discusses several other design issues such as VTP, port configurations, and passwords.

CHAPTER 3

Campus Design Implementation

This chapter is designed to be a compendium of best practice for campus design. It draws on the collective wisdom of many people and many attempts at achieving the elusive goal of a perfect campus design. It is intended to be a concentrated shot of what has been proven to work well, and what has been proven to be a flop. The hope is that it will serve not only as an eye-opener, but as something that you will return to whenever you face campus design decisions.

The material in other chapters has, in some form, implied many of the items discussed in this chapter. Therefore, this chapter does not attempt to fully explain the background of every point (that is the job of the previous 14 chapters!). Instead, each point is fairly concise and uses references and pointers to other chapters for more detail.

VLANs

When the word *switching* is brought up, the first thing that comes to most network engineer's minds is the subject of VLANs. The use of VLANs can make or break a campus design. This section discusses some of the most important issues to remember when designing and implementing VLANs in your network.

The Appropriate Use of VLANs

Given that VLANs are associated so closely with switching, people most often think of what Chapter 14, "Campus Design Models," of *Cisco LAN Switching* referred to as campus-wide VLANs. Given the popularity of campus-wide VLANs as both a concept and a design, this section discusses its pro and cons, as well as an alternate design for consideration.

The popularity of campus-wide VLANs is due in large part to several well-publicized benefits to this approach. First, it can allow direct Layer 2 paths between all of the devices located in the same community of interest. By doing so, this can remove routers from the path of high-volume traffic such as that going to a departmental file server. Assuming that software-based routers are in use, there is the potential for a tremendous increase in available bandwidth.

Second, campus-wide VLANs make it possible to use technology like Cisco's User Registration Tool (URT). By functioning as a sophisticated extension to the VLAN membership policy server (VMPS) technology discussed in Chapter 5, "VLANs," of *Cisco LAN Switching*, URT allows VLAN placement to be transparently determined by authentication servers such as Windows NT Domain Controllers and NetWare Directory Services (NDS). Organizations such as universities have found this feature very appealing because they can create one or more VLANs for professors and administrative staff while creating separate VLANs for students. Consequently, the same physical campus infrastructure can be used to logically segregate the student traffic while still allowing the use of roving laptop users.

The third benefit of campus-wide VLANs is actually implied by the second benefit— campus-wide VLANs allow these roving users to be controlled by a centralized set of access lists. For example, a university using campus-wide VLANs might utilize a pair of 7500 routers located in the data center for all inter-VLAN routing. As a result, access lists between the VLANs only need to be configured in two places. Consider the alternative where routers (or Layer 3 switches) might be deployed in every building on campus. To maintain user mobility, each of these routers needs to be configured with all of the VLANs and access lists used throughout the entire campus. This can obviously lead to a situation where potentially hundreds of access lists must be maintained.

TIP   Although campus-wide VLANs have several well-publicized benefits and are quite popular, they create many network design and management issues. Try to avoid using campus-wide VLANs.

Although these advantages are very alluring, many organizations that implement this approach quickly discover their downsides. Most of the disadvantages are the result of one characteristic of campus-wide VLANs: a lack of hierarchy. Specifically, this lack of hierarchy creates significant scalability problems that can affect the network's stability and maintainability. Furthermore, these problems are often difficult to troubleshoot because of the dynamic and non-deterministic nature of campus-wide VLANs (not to mention that it can be difficult to know where to start troubleshooting in a flat network). For more information on these issues, please refer to Chapter 14, "Campus Design Models," Chapter 11, "Layer 3 Switching," and Chapter 17, "Case Studies: Implementing Switches," of *Cisco LAN Switching*.

Although many books and vendors discuss campus-wide VLANs as simply the way to use switching, Layer 3 switching introduces a completely different approach that is definitely worthy of consideration. Chapter 14 of *Cisco LAN Switching* discussed these Layer 3 approaches under the heading of the multilayer campus design model. Although this approach cannot match the support for centralized access lists available under campus-wide VLANs, it can allow you to build and maintain much larger networks than is typically possible with campus-wide VLANs. Layer 3 switching can also be used with the Dynamic Host Control Protocol (DHCP), a very proven and scalable technique for handling user mobility (see the next section). Therefore, as a general rule of thumb, use the multilayer model as your default design choice and only use flat earth designs if there is a compelling reason to justify the risks. For more information on the advantages and implementation details of the multilayer model, see Chapter 11, Chapter 14, and Chapter 17 of *Cisco LAN Switching*.

Note that this implies a fundamental difference in how VLANs are used between the two design models. In the case of campus-wide VLANs, VLANs are used to create logical partitions unique to the entire campus network. In the case of the multilayer model, they are used to create logical partitions that may be unique to a single IDF/access layer wiring closet.

TIP   The multilayer design model uses VLANs in a completely different fashion from the campus-wide VLANs model. In the multilayer model, VLANs are very often only unique to a single IDF device whereas campus-wide VLANs are globally unique.

Use DHCP to Solve User Mobility Problems

Many network engineers feel that campus-wide VLANs are the only way to handle mobile users and unwittingly saddle themselves with a flat network that requires high maintenance. As mentioned in the previous section, many user-mobility problems can be solved with DHCP. Because DHCP fits well into hierarchical designs that utilize Layer 3 processing for scalability, it can be a much safer choice than using campus-wide VLANs. As discussed in Chapter 11 and Chapter 17 in *Cisco LAN Switching*, the use of DHCP simply requires one or more **ip helper-address** statements on each router (or Layer 3 switch) interface. When using IP helper addresses for DHCP, consider using the **no ip forward-protocol** command to disable the forwarding of unwanted traffic types that are enabled by default (the **ip helper-address** command automatically enables forwarding of the following UDP ports: 37, 49, 53, 67, 68, 69, 137, and 138). Most commonly, UDP ports 137 and 138 are removed to prevent excessive forwarding of NetBIOS name registration traffic.

TIP   Be careful to not simply enter **no ip forward-protocol upd**. Prior to 12.0, entering this command disabled *all* of the default UDP ports, including ports 67 and 68 that are used by DHCP. Although **no ip forward-protocol upd** does not disable DHCP in early releases of 12.0, proceed with caution. For an example of **ip helper-address** and **no ip forward-protocol**, see Chapter 17 of *Cisco LAN Switching*.

VLAN Numbering

Although VLAN numbering is a very simple task, having a well thought-out plan can help make the network easier to understand and manage in the long run. In general, there are two approaches to VLAN numbering:

* Globally-unique VLAN numbers
* Pattern-based VLAN numbers

In globally-unique VLAN numbers, every VLAN has a unique numeric identifier. For example, consider the network shown in Figure 3-1. Here, the VLANs in Building 1 use numbers 10–13, Building 2 uses 20–23, and Building 3 uses 30–33.

Figure 3-1 *Globally-Unique VLANs*

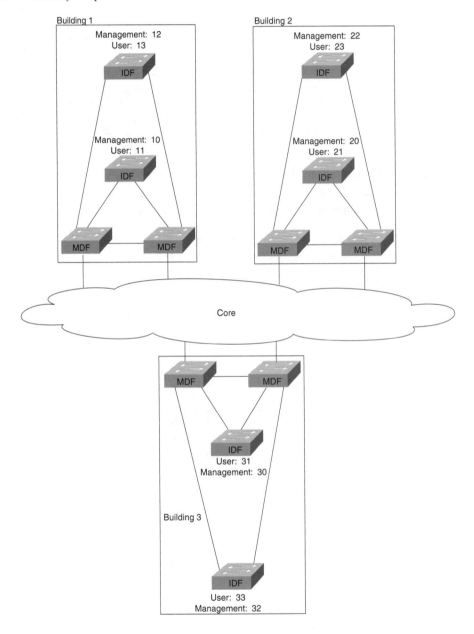

When using globally-unique VLANs, try to establish an easily remembered scheme such as the one used in Figure 3-1 (Building 1 uses VLANs 1X, Building 2 uses 2X, and so on).

In the case of pattern-based VLAN numbers, the same VLAN number is used for the same purpose in each building. For example, Figure 3-2 shows a network where the management VLAN is always 1, the first end user VLAN is 2, the second end user VLAN is 3, and so on.

Figure 3-2   *Pattern-Based VLANs*

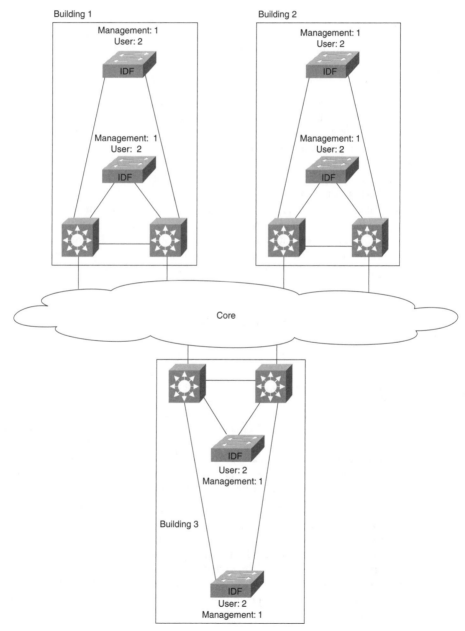

Which approach you use is primarily driven by what type of design model you adopt. If you have utilized the campus-wide VLANs model, you are essentially forced to use globally-unique VLAN numbers. Although there are special cases and "hacks" where this may not be true, not using unique VLANs in flat designs can lead to cross-mapped VLANs and widespread connectivity problems.

TIP	Use globally-unique VLAN numbers with campus-wide VLANs.

If you are using the multilayer model, either numbering scheme can be adopted. Because VLANs are terminated at MDF/distribution layer switches, there is no underlying technical requirement that the VLAN numbers must match (this is especially true when using using switching router platforms such as the Catalyst 8500). In fact, even if the VLAN numbers do match, they are still maintained as completely separate broadcast domains because of Layer 3 switching/routing. If you like the simplicity of knowing that the management VLAN is always VLAN 1, the pattern-based approach might be more appropriate. On the other hand, some organizations prefer to keep every VLAN number unique just as every IP subnet is unique (this approach often ties the VLAN number to the subnet number—for example, VLAN 25 might be 10.1.25.0/24). In other cases, a blend of the two numbering schemes works best. Here, organizations typically adopt a single number for use in all management VLANs but use unique numbers for end-user VLANs.

TIP	The multilayer model can be used with both globally-unique VLANs and pattern-based VLANs.

Use Meaningful VLAN Names

Although common sense dictates that clearly-named VLANs serve as a form of documentation, networks are frequently built with useless VLAN names. Recall from Chapter 5 of *Cisco LAN Switching* that if you do not specify a VLAN name, the Catalysts use a very creative name such as VLAN0002 for VLAN 2 and VLAN0003 for VLAN3. In other cases, organizations do specify a VLAN name as a parameter to the **set vlan** command, but the names are cryptic or poorly maintained.

It is usually a far better choice to create VLAN names that actually describe the function of that broadcast domain. This is especially true when using campus-wide VLANs and globally-unique VLAN numbers. The dynamic and non-hierarchical nature of these networks makes troubleshooting challenging enough without having to waste time trying to determine what VLAN a problem involves. Having clearly-defined and descriptive VLAN names can save critical time during a network outage (as well as avoiding the confusion that might cause an administrator to misconfigure a device and thus *create* a network outage).

TIP	Descriptive VLAN names are especially important when using campus-wide VLANs.

Although VLAN names are less important when the multilayer design model is in use, the names should at least differentiate management and end-user traffic. Try to include the name of the department or IDF/access layer closet where the VLAN is used. Also, some organizations like to include the IP subnet number in the VLAN name.

Use Separate Management VLANs

When first exposed to VLANs, many network administrators find them confusing and therefore decide to adopt a policy of placing only a single VLAN on every switch. Although this can have an appealing simplicity, it can seriously destabilize your network. In short, you want to always use at least two VLANs on every Layer 2 Catalyst switch. At a minimum, you want one VLAN for management traffic and a separate VLAN for end-user traffic.

TIP	Make sure every Layer 2 switch participates in at least two VLANs: one that functions as the management VLAN and one or more for end-user VLANs.

However, this is not to suggest that having more than two VLANs is a good idea. To the contrary, the simplicity of maintaining a single end-user VLAN (or at least a small number) can be very beneficial for network maintenance.

Why, then, is it so important to have at least two VLANs? Think back to the material discussed in Chapter 5 of *Cisco LAN Switching* regarding the impact of broadcasts on end stations. Because broadcasts are not filtered by hardware on-board the network interface card (NIC), every broadcast is passed up to Layer 3 using an interrupt to the central CPU. The more time that the CPU spends looking at unwanted broadcast packets, the less time it has for more useful tasks (like playing Doom!).

Well, the CPU on a Catalyst's Supervisor is no different. The CPU must inspect every broadcast packet to determine if it is an ARP destined for its IP address or some other interesting broadcast packet. However, if the level of uninteresting traffic becomes too large, the CPU can become overwhelmed and start dropping packets. If it drops Doom packets, no harm is done. On the other hand, if it drops Spanning Tree BPDUs, the whole network could destabilize.

NOTE
Note that this section is referring to Layer 2 Catalysts such as the 2900s, 4000s, 5000s, and 6000s. Because these devices currently have one IP address that is only assigned to a single VLAN, the selection of this VLAN can be important. On the other hand, this point generally does not apply to router-like Catalysts such as the 8500. Because these platforms generally have an IP address assigned to *every* VLAN, trying to pick the best VLAN for an IP address obviously becomes irrelevant. For more information on the Catalyst 8500, see Chapter 11 of *Cisco LAN Switching*.

In fact, this Spanning Tree problem is one of the more common issues in flat earth campus networks. The story usually goes something like this: The network is humming along fine until a burst of broadcast data in the management VLAN causes a switch to become overwhelmed to the point where is starts dropping packets. Because some of these packets are BPDUs, the switch falls behind in its Spanning Tree information and inadvertently creates a Layer 2 loop in the network. At this point, the broadcasts in the network go into a full feedback loop as discussed in Chapter 6, "Understanding Spanning Tree," of *Cisco LAN Switching*.

If this loop occurs in one or more VLANs other than the management VLAN, it can quickly starve out all remaining trunk bandwidth throughout the entire campus in a flat network. However, the Supervisor CPUs are insulated by the VLAN switching ASICs and continue operating normally (recall that all data forwarding is handled by ASICs in Catalyst gear).

On the other hand, if the loop occurs in the management VLAN (the VLAN where SC0 is assigned), the results can be truly catastrophic. Suddenly, every switch CPU is hit with a tidal wave of broadcast traffic, completely crushing every switch in a downward spiral that virtually eliminates any chance of the network recovering from this problem. If a network is utilizing campus-wide VLANs, this problem can spread to every switch within a matter of seconds.

NOTE
Recall that SC0 is the management interface used in Catalyst switches such as the 4000s, 5000s, and 6000s. This is where the management IP address is assigned to a Catalyst Supervisor. Because the CPU processes all broadcast packets (and some multicast packets) received on this interface, it is important to not overwhelm the CPU.

How do you know if your CPU is struggling to keep up with traffic in the network? First, you can use the Catalyst 5000 **show inband** command (this is used for Supervisor IIIs; use **show biga** on Supervisor Is and IIs [biga stands for Backplane Interface Gate Array]) to display low-level statistics for the device. Look under the **Receive** section for the **RsrcErrors** field. This lists the number of received frames that were dropped by the CPU. Second, to view the load directly on the CPU, use the undocumented command **ps -c**. The final line of this display lists the CPU *idle* time (subtract from 100 to calculate the load). Note that **ps-c** has been replaced by **show proc cpu** in newer images.

TIP
Use the **show inband**, **show biga**, **ps -c**, and **show proc cpu** commands to determine if your CPU is overloaded.

If you find that you are facing a problem of CPU overload, also read the section "Consider Using Loop-Free Management VLANs" later in this chapter.

Deciding What Number Should be Used for the Management VLAN

A common question surrounds the issue of VLAN numbering for the management VLAN. To appropriately answer this question, you must consider the three types of traffic that pass through Catalyst switches:

- Control traffic
- Management traffic
- End-user traffic

Control traffic encompasses plug and play-oriented protocols such as DISL/DTP (used for trunk state negotiation), CDP, PAgP, and VTP. *These protocols always use VLAN 1.*

Management traffic includes end-to-end and IP-based protocols such as Telnet, SNMP, and VQP (the protocol used by VMPS). *These protocols always use the VLAN assign to SC0.*

End-user traffic is all of the remaining traffic on your network. Obviously, this represents the majority of traffic on most networks.

The overriding principle concerning Management VLAN design is to *never mix end-user traffic with the control and management traffic*. Failing to abide by this rule will open your network up to the sort of network meltdown scenarios discussed in the previous section.

TIP   Never mix end-user traffic with control and management traffic.

When implementing this principle, you must generally choose one of two designs:

- Use VLAN 1 for all control *and* management traffic while placing end-user traffic in other VLANs (VLANs 2–1000).
- Use VLAN 1 for control traffic, another VLAN (such as VLAN 2) for management traffic, and the remaining VLAN for end-user traffic (such as VLAN 3–1000).

The first option combines control and management traffic in VLAN 1. The advantage of this approach is management simplicity (it is the default setting and uses a single VLAN). The primary disadvantage of this approach centers around the default behavior of VLAN 1—because VLAN 1 cannot currently be removed from trunk links, it is easy for this VLAN to become extremely large. For example, the use of Ethernet trunks throughout a network along with MLS Layer 3 switching in the MDF/distribution layer will result in VLAN 1 spanning *every* link and every switch in the campus, exactly what you do *not* want for your all-important management VLAN. Therefore, placing SC0 in such as large and flat VLAN can be risky.

NOTE	Although VLAN 1 cannot be removed from Ethernet trunks in current versions of Catalyst code, Cisco is developing a feature that will provide this capability in the future. In short, this feature is expected to allow VLAN 1 to be removed from both trunk links and the VTP VLAN database. Therefore, from a user-interface perspective, enabling this feature effectively removes VLAN 1 from the device. However, from the point of view of the Catalyst internals, the VLAN will actually remain in use, but only for control traffic such as VTP and CDP (for example, a Sniffer will reveal these packets tagged with a VLAN 1 header on trunk links). In other words, this feature will essentially convert VLAN 1 into a "reserved" VLAN than can only be used for control traffic.

This risk can be avoided with the second option where the control and management traffic are separated. Whereas the control traffic must use VLAN 1, the management traffic is relocated to a different VLAN (many organizations choose to use VLAN 2, 999, or 1000). As a result, SC0 and the CPU will be insulated from potential broadcast problems in VLAN 1. This optimization can be particularly important in extremely large campus networks that are lacking in Layer 3 hierarchy.

TIP	For the most conservative management/control VLAN design, only use VLAN 1 for control traffic while placing SC0 in its own VLAN (in other words, no end-user traffic will use this VLAN).
	Also, when using the upcoming feature that "removes" VLAN 1 from a Catalyst, you are effectively forced to use this approach.

Be Careful When Moving SC0's VLAN

Although some traffic always uses VLAN 1, other management traffic changes VLANs as SC0 is reassigned. This includes all of the end-to-end protocols (as opposed to the link-by-link protocols that only use VLAN 1) such as:

- Telnet
- SNMP
- The VQP protocol used by VMPS
- Syslog
- Ping

For these protocols to function, SC0 must be assigned to the correct VLAN with a valid IP address and one or more functioning default gateways to reach the rest of the network. The most common problem here is that people often move SC0 to a different VLAN for troubleshooting purposes and forget to move it back when they are done. Although this can help troubleshoot the immediate problem, it is almost guaranteed to create more problems! Another common problem is failing to use an IP address that is appropriate for the VLAN assigned to SC0.

TIP	If you reconfigure SC0 for troubleshooting (or other) purposes, be sure to return it to its original state.

Prune VLANs from Trunks

Two generic technologies are available for creating trunks that share multiple VLANs:

- Implicit tagging
- Explicit tagging

When using implicit tagging, some information already contained in the frame serves as an indicator of VLAN membership. Many vendors have created equipment that uses MAC addresses for this purpose (other possibilities include Layer 3 addresses or Layer 4 port numbers). The downside of this approach is that you must devise some technique for sharing these tags. For example, when using MAC addresses, all of the switches must be told what VLAN every MAC address has been assigned to. Maintaining and synchronizing these potentially huge tables can be a real problem.

To avoid these synchronization issues, Cisco has adopted the approach of using explicit tagging through ISL and 802.1Q. There are two advantages to explicit tagging. First, because the tag is carried in an extra header field that is added to the original frame, VLAN membership becomes completely unambiguous (therefore preventing problems associated with frames bleeding through between VLANs). Second, each switch needs to know only the VLAN assignments of its directly-connected ports (in implicit tagging, the shared tables require every switch to maintain knowledge of every MAC address/end station). As a result, the amount of state information required by each switch is dramatically reduced.

NOTE	Cisco's use of explicit tagging creates significant scalability benefits.

However, there is a hidden downside to the advantage of every switch not needing to know what VLANs other switches are using—flooded traffic must be sent to every switch in the Layer 2 network. In other words, by default, one copy of every broadcast, multicast, and unknown unicast frame is flooded across every trunk link in a Layer 2 domain.

Two approaches can be used to reduce the impact of this flooding. First, note that if you are using campus-wide VLANs, this flooding problem also becomes campus-wide. Therefore, one of the simplest and most scalable ways to reduce this flooding is to partition the network with several Layer 3 barriers that utilize routing (Layer 3 switching) technology. This breaks the network into smaller Layer 2 pockets and constrains the flooding to each pocket.

Where Layer 3 switching cannot prevent unnecessary flooding (such as with campus-wide VLANs or within each of the Layer 2 pockets created by Layer 3 switching), a second technique of VLAN pruning can be employed. By using the **clear trunk** command discussed in Chapter 8, "Trunking Technologies and Applications," of *Cisco LAN Switching*, unused VLANs can be manually pruned from a trunk. Therefore, when a given switch needs to flood a frame, it only sends it out access ports locally assigned to the source VLAN and trunk links that have not been pruned of this VLAN. For example, an MDF switch can be configured to flood frames only for VLANs 1 and 2 to a given IDF switch if the switch only participates in these two VLANs. To automate the process of pruning, VTP pruning can be used. For more information on VTP pruning, please refer to Chapter 12, "VLAN Trunking Protocol," of *Cisco LAN Switching*

One of the most important uses of manual VLAN pruning involves the use of a Layer 2 campus core, the subject of the next section.

TIP   VLAN pruning on trunk lines is one of the most important keys to the successful implementation of a network containing Layer 2 Catalyst switching.

Make Layer 2 Cores Loop Free

When using a Layer 2 core in association with the multilayer model, strive to eliminate links that create loops. On one hand, this sounds completely counter-intuitive. After all, most network engineers spend countless hours trying to improve the resiliency of their network's core. However, by carefully pruning your network of certain links and VLANs, you can eliminate Spanning Tree convergence delays while still maintaining a high degree of redundancy and network resiliency. In other words, simply throwing more links (and VLANs) at a Layer 2 core can actually *degrade* network reliability by introducing Spanning Tree delays.

Furthermore, there is another advantage to using loop-free Layer 2 cores. When loops exist, Spanning Tree automatically places ports in the Blocking state and therefore reduces the capability to load balance across the core. By eliminating loops and therefore removing Spanning Tree Blocking ports, every path through the core can be utilized to maximize available bandwidth in this important area of the network.

For example, consider the collapsed Layer 2 backbone illustrated in Figure 3-3.

Figure 3-3   *A Loop-Free Collapsed Layer 2 Core*

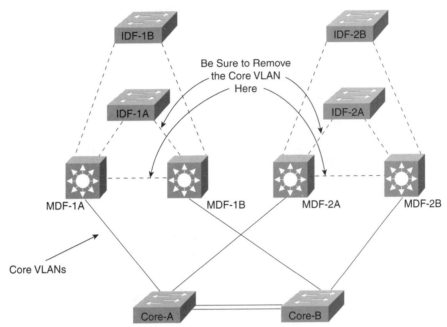

The core in Figure 3-3 is formed by a pair of redundant Layer 2 switches each carrying a single VLAN. All four of the MDF switches connect to one of the core switches (Core-A or Core-B), allowing any single link or switch to fail without creating a permanent outage. If the four MDF switches are configured with Catalyst 8500-style switching routers, then this will automatically result in a loop-free core. On the other hand, the use of Layer 3 router switching (MLS) in the MDF devices requires more careful planning. Specially, the core VLAN must be removed from the links to IDF switches as well as on the link between MDF switches.

TIP	When using MLS (and other forms of routing switches), be certain that you remove the core VLAN from links within the distribution block (the triangles of connectivity formed by MDF and IDF switches).

Larger Layer 2 campus cores require even more careful planning. For example, Figure 3-4 shows a network that covers a larger geographic area and therefore uses four Layer 2 switches within the core. This design is often referred to as a "split Layer 2" core.

Figure 3-4 *A Split Layer 2 Core*

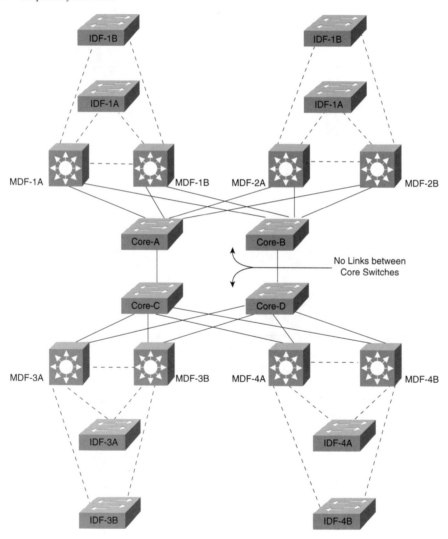

In this case, the key to creating a fast-converging and resilient core is to actually partition the core into two separate VLANs and not cross-link the switches to each other. The first core VLAN is used for the pair of switches on the left, and the second VLAN is used for the pair of switches on the right. If the core switches in Figure 3-4 were cross-linked or fully meshed and a single VLAN were deployed, Spanning Tree convergence and load balancing issues would become a problem.

Finally, notice that creating a loop-free core requires the use of Layer 3 switching in the MDF/distribution layer closets. When using campus-wide VLANs, the only way to achieve a loop-free core is to remove all loops from the *entire* network, obviously a risky endeavor if you are at all concerned about redundancy. Again, follow the suggestion of this chapter's first section and try to always use the multilayer model and the scalability benefits it achieves through the use of Layer 3 switching.

TIP	When using split Layer 2 cores, some network designers chose to use this to segregate the traffic by protocol to provide additional control. For example, the Core-A and Core-C switches could be used for IP traffic while the Core-B and Core-D can carry IPX traffic. This can be a useful way of guaranteeing a certain amount of bandwidth for each protocol. It is especially useful when you have non-routable protocols that require bridging throughout a large section of the network. This will allow one half of the core to carry the non-routable/bridged traffic while the other half carries the multiprotocol routed traffic.

This section has repeatedly discussed the pruning of VLANs from links. Obviously, one way to accomplish this is to use the **clear trunk** command discussed in the "Restricting VLANs on a Trunk" section of Chapter 8 of *Cisco LAN Switching*. However, the simplest and most effective approach for removing VLANs from a campus core is to just use non-trunk links. By merely assigning these ports to the core VLAN, you will automatically prevent VLANs from spanning the core and creating flat earth VLANs.

TIP	Use non-trunk links in the campus core to avoid campus-wide end-user VLANs.

In fact, this technique is also the most effective method of removing VLAN 1 from the core. Recall that current versions of Catalyst code do not allow you to prune VLAN 1 from Ethernet trunks. Therefore, as discussed earlier, this can result in a single campus-wide VLAN in the all-important VLAN 1 (the *last* place you want to have loops and broadcast problems).

TIP	Use non-trunk links in the campus core to avoid a campus-wide VLAN in VLAN 1 (this is where you least want a flat earth VLAN, especially if SC0 is assign to VLAN 1).

Don't Forget PLANs

When creating a new design or when your first one or two attempts at solving a particular problem fail, redraw your VLAN design using physical LANs (PLANs). In other words, take the logical topology created through the use of virtual LANs and redraw it using PLANs.

PLAN is a somewhat tongue-in-cheek term the author coined to describe a very serious issue. For some reason, the human brain is almost guaranteed to forget all knowledge of IP subnetting when faced with virtual LANs. People spend days looking at Sniffer traces of complex things like ISL trunks and Spanning Tree to only learn in the end that someone "fat fingered" one digit in an IP address.

So, you ask, what the heck is a PLAN? To answer this mystery, first consider Figure 3-5, a drawing of a typical network using VLANs.

Figure 3-5   *Virtual LANs (VLANs)*

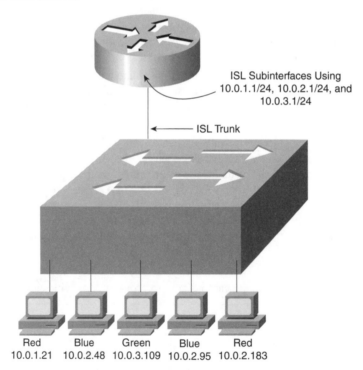

Figure 3-6 redraws Figure 3-5 using PLANs.

Figure 3-6   *Physical LANs (PLANs)*

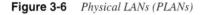
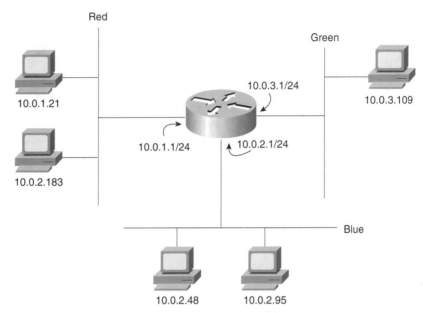

Each VLAN in Figure 3-6 has been redrawn as a separate segment connected to a different router interface. It depicts the logical separation of VLANs with the physical separation used in traditional router and hub designs. However, from a Layer 3 perspective, both networks are identical.

By doing this, it makes the network extremely easy to understand. In fact, it makes it painfully obvious that this network contains a problem—the host using 10.0.2.183 is located on the wrong segment/VLAN (it should be on the Blue VLAN).

Although this might seem like a simple example, simple addressing issues trip up even the best of us from time to time. Why not use a technique that removes VLANs as an extra layer of obfuscation? However, PLANs can be useful in many situations other than for your own troubleshooting. Even if you understand why a network is having a problem, PLANs can be useful for explaining it to other people who might not see the problem as clearly. PLANs can also be used to simplify a new design and help you better analyze the traffic flows and any potential problems.

TIP   PLANs are no joke—use them to help troubleshoot and explain your network.

How to Handle Non-Routable Protocols

Chapter 11 of *Cisco LAN Switching* discussed various approaches to integrating Layer 3 routing with Layer 2 bridging, including options such as bridging between VLANs, Concurrent Routing and Bridging (CRB), and Integrated Routing and Bridging (IRB). Most organizations utilize one of these techniques because of the need to have users in two different VLANs communicate via a non-routable protocol such as NetBEUI or LAT. Although the techniques discussed in Chapter 11 of *Cisco LAN Switching* can provide relief in limited situations, it is almost always better to avoid their use entirely. Instead, try to place all users of a particular non-routable protocol in a single VLAN. In situations where Catalyst 8500-style switching routers are in use, this might require IRB to be enabled (the Layer 2 nature of MLS does not require the use of IRB).

For more information, see the "Integration Between Routing and Bridging" section in Chapter 11 of *Cisco LAN Switching*.

TIP   Try to avoid "bridging between VLANs" at all costs.

Spanning Tree

Intertwined with the issue of VLANs is the subject of the Spanning-Tree Protocol. In fact, it is the inappropriate use of VLANs (the flat earth theory) that most often leads to Spanning Tree problems in the first place. This section discusses some of the dos and don'ts of the Spanning-Tree Protocol.

One of the primary themes developed throughout this section is that although Spanning Tree can be quite manageable when used in conjunction with Layer 3 switching, it can also become very complex when used in large, flat designs like campus-wide VLANs. Combining good Spanning Tree knowledge with a good design is the key to success.

Keep Spanning Tree Domains Small

One of the most effective techniques for minimizing Spanning Tree problems is keeping Spanning Tree domains small in size. The easiest way to accomplish this is to use the multilayer design model. By automatically creating Layer 3 barriers that partition the network from a Spanning Tree point of view, most of the typical Spanning Tree problems become non-issues.

There are many benefits to constricting Spanning Tree to small pockets within your network, including the following:

* It allows you to safely tune the Spanning Tree timers.

* As a result, Spanning Tree convergence time can be significantly improved.

* It becomes very difficult for Spanning Tree problems in one section of the network to spread to other sections of the network.

- When using the switching router (Catalyst 8500) form of the multilayer design model, Spanning Tree load balancing can be eliminated. In this case, the IDF traffic creates *Layer 2 V's* that are inherently loop free and therefore do not require the Spanning-Tree Protocol, although I recommend that you don't disable Spanning Tree; see the next section.

Note   If you enable bridging and/or IRB on Catalyst 8500 devices, they will starting bridging traffic and convert the Layer 2 V's that they produce by default into Layer 2 triangles. This will obviously require the use of Spanning Tree (use of the Root Bridge placement technique discussed in the following bullet point is recommended).

- When using the routing switch (MLS) form of the multilayer design model, Spanning Tree load balancing can be dramatically simplified through the use of the Root Bridge placement technique. When using MLS and the multilayer model, each IDF and a pair of MDFs create *Layer 2 triangles* that, although not loop free, are easy to manage. For more information on the Root Bridge placement approach to Spanning Tree load balancing, see Chapter 7, "Advanced Spanning Tree," and Chapter 17 of *Cisco LAN Switching*.
- Spanning Tree becomes much simpler to design, document, and understand.
- Troubleshooting becomes much easier.

Figure 3-7 illustrates the Layer 2 triangles created by MLS (Part A) and the Layer 2 V's created by switching routers. Although MLS very often uses route-switch modules (RSMs), a logical representation has been used for Part A.

Figure 3-7   *Layer 2 Topologies under Routing Switches (MLS) and Switching Routers*

Part A: Routing Switch (MLS)

Part B: Switching Router (8500)

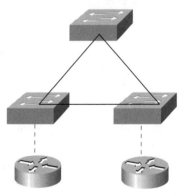

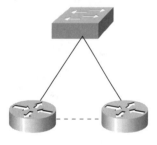

Layer 3 Switches Are Configured as Routers

NOTE   It is important to realize that both routing switches (MLS) and switching routers (8500s) can be used to create the designs shown in Figure 3-7. This section is merely trying to point out the *default* behavior and most common use of these platforms.

When using campus-wide VLANs, it is often possible to achieve some of the benefits listed in this section by manually pruning VLANs from selected trunks. However, it is not possible to create the simplicity and scalability that are available when using Layer 3 switching. Also, the pruning action can often reduce redundancy in the network.

The multilayer model allows the benefits listed in this section to be easily designed into the network. When using routing switches (MLS) as shown in Part A, this can be accomplished by pruning selected VLANs from key trunk links (such as links in the core and between MDF switches). When using switching routers such as the 8500 as shown in Part B, the benefits of having small Spanning Tree domains accrue by default.

Don't Disable Spanning Tree

In frustration, many organizations disable the Spanning-Tree Protocol to achieve network stability (especially when using flat earth designs). However, when this is done at the expense of redundancy, it obviously introduces a whole new set of problems.

When Spanning Tree is disabled, you are not protected from the inevitable configuration mistakes that create Layer 2 loops in the network. As discussed in Chapter 6 of *Cisco LAN Switching*, Layer 2 protocols have no way of recovering from feedback loops without a protocol such as Spanning Tree (there is no Time To Live [TTL] field in Layer 2 headers)—the loop continues until you manually intervene.

Typically, Spanning Tree is disabled in one of three situations:

- **As a last resort to achieve network stability under the campus-wide VLANs design model**—However, because this also requires that redundancy be eliminated, this is not recommended.

- **When using Catalyst 8500-style switching routers in the MDF/distribution layer closets**—Because switching routers result in loop-free Layer 2 V's (as shown in Part B of Figure 3-7), Spanning Tree is no longer required—at least for the intended topology. However, loops can be formed unintentionally through configuration and cabling mistakes on the part of network administrators or because end users installed devices such as hubs or switches. Therefore, an element of risk remains with this approach.

- **When using a LANE backbone**—Because LANE automatically creates a loop-free topology *within the ATM core itself*, Spanning Tree can be disabled. In fact, ATM-centric vendors such as Fore Systems disable Spanning Tree for LANE by default. However, you must be careful to not create Layer 2 loops *outside* the LANE backbone. Not only does this include the examples discussed in the previous bullet, it also includes such practices as using redundant Ethernet links to extend the ATM backbone to IDF wiring closets.

In general, it is better to use scalable design techniques and Spanning Tree tuning rather than to disable the Spanning-Tree Protocol altogether. As discussed in the previous section, designs such as the multilayer model can achieve network stability without having to resort to disabling Spanning Tree. Also, a carefully planned design can then allow Spanning Tree to be tuned for better performance.

Evaluate Spanning Tree Patterns

As discussed in Chapter 11 and Chapter 14 of *Cisco LAN Switching*, using Layer 3 switching and the multilayer design model generally results in networks that are comprised of many small "triangles" and "V's" of Layer 2 connectivity.

As this material discussed, switching router platforms such as the Catalyst 8500s produce Layer 2 V's by default. Although bridging and IRB can be enabled to convert these V's into Layer 2 triangles, it is generally advisable to avoid widespread deployment of these features (see the section "Integration between Routing and Bridging" in Chapter 11 of *Cisco LAN Switching*). Therefore, you will usually see Layer 2 V's in conjunction with switching router technology.

From a Spanning Tree perspective, it is important to note that these V's are loop-free and therefore do not place any ports in the blocking state. As a result, Spanning Tree will not impact your failover performance.

NOTE	Although Spanning Tree will not impact failover performance of the IDF uplink ports when using Layer 2 Vs, it is still enabled by default and may impact end-user devices. Therefore, you may wish to configure PortFast on end-user ports to facilitate start-up protocols such as DHCP and NetWare authentication.

Unlike 8500s where Layer 2 V's are far more common, MLS (and routing switches) allow you to easily configure either Layer 2 triangles *or* V's. By default, MLS allows all VLANs to transit the switch. Therefore, assuming that you have removed end-user VLANs from the network core, you will be left with Layer 2 triangles by default (Part A of Figure 3-7). However, by pruning a given VLAN from the link between the MDF/distribution switches, this VLAN can easily be converted into a V (Part B of Figure 3-7). In other words, by simply pruning the VLAN from the triangle's base, it is converted into a V.

From a Spanning Tree perspective, it is important to evaluate the differences that this brings to your network. If you opt for using triangles, then Spanning Tree will be in full effect. The Root Bridge placement form of load balancing and features such as UplinkFast will be important. If you opt for the Layer 2 V's, you will be left with the same "almost Spanning Tree free" situation described several paragraphs earlier in connection with the 8500s.

TIP Be sure to consider the impact and performance of Spanning Tree where you have Layer 2 triangles in your campus network.

Consider Using Switching Routers to Virtually Eliminate Spanning Tree

Because Catalyst 8500-style switching routers in the MDF/distribution layer closets eliminates loops through the IDF switches, this results in Layer 2 V's. Therefore, Spanning Tree can be much simpler to design, maintain, and troubleshoot. The IDF switch automatically elects itself as the Root Bridge of a one-bridge network (the Layer 3 switches prevent the bridges from learning about each other and keep the Spanning Tree separate). Timer values can be fairly aggressively tuned without risk (use the **set spantree root** command with a diameter of 2 or 3 hops). Also, Spanning Tree load balancing is no longer necessary.

NOTE Note that Layer 2 V's can also be created with routing switch (MLS) platforms by pruning VLAN from selected links (in this case, the base of the triangle—the MDF-to-MDF link).

Consider Using Loop-Free Management VLANs

As discussed in the section "Use Separate Management VLANs," exposing a Layer 2 Catalyst Supervisor to excessive broadcast traffic can lead to network-wide outages. This section recommended using a management VLAN to isolate the Catalyst SC0 interface from end-user broadcast traffic. However, even when using a separate management VLAN, some risk remains. If a loop were to form in the management VLAN itself, the Supervisors could once again find themselves crushed by a wave of traffic.

TIP Make certain that your design minimizes the risk of braodcast storms occurring in the management VLAN.

Therefore, ensuring that the management VLAN itself is loop free can provide an additional layer of protection. In general, two techniques can be used to create a loop-free management VLAN:

- The use of Catalyst 8500-style switching routers in the MDF/distribution layer automatically creates loop-free management VLANs on the IDF/access devices by default. Notice that this also implies that you should not use IRB to merge the management VLANs back into a single VLAN. Although this can appear to simplify the management of your network by placing all of the switches in a single VLAN, it can create management problems in the long term by adding loops into the management VLAN.

- Campus-wide VLANs often require the use of an out-of-band management network. Because it is very difficult to maintain a loop free and stable environment when campus-wide VLANs are in use, you often have to resort to running separate Ethernet links from routers to a port on each Catalyst. By then assigning only this Ethernet port to the management VLAN used for SC0, a loop-free topology can be created. The ME1 (Management Ethernet) ports available on some Catalyst devices can also be used to create an out-of-band management network.

Figure 3-8 illustrates a typical network using the out-of-band approach to creating loop-free management VLANs. Assume that because the switches are deployed in a haphazard manner, it is not feasible to create loop-free management VLANs using the existing infrastructure. Instead, separate Ethernet links are pulled from the nearest available router port. Where possible, hubs can be used to reduce the number of router ports required.

Figure 3-8   *Creating Loop-Free Management VLANs with an Out-Of-Band Network*

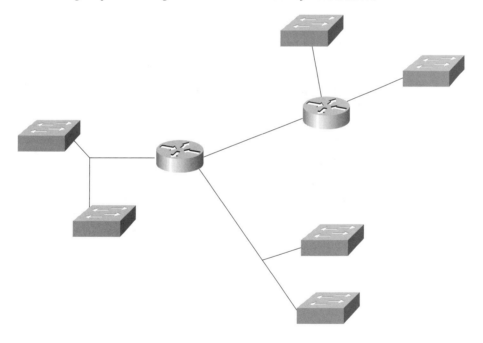

As discussed in the section "Make Layer 2 Cores Loop-Free," you should also keep an eye on VLAN 1. Although you may have carefully used Layer 3 switching to create hierarchy in your network, you can still be left with a campus-wide VLAN in VLAN 1 (especially if you are using MLS Layer 3 switching). Note that this will be true even if you followed the earlier advice (see the section "Prune VLANs from Trunks") of pruning VLANs core VLANs from the wiring closet trunks and wiring closet VLANs from the core trunks (recall that VLAN 1 *cannot be deleted* and *cannot be pruned* from Ethernet trunk links in current code images).

Because VLAN 1 is given special priority because of the control traffic discussed in the section "Deciding What Number Should be Used for the Management VLAN," a broadcast loop in this VLAN can be devastating to the health of your network. How, then, are you supposed to control this situation? In general, organizations have used one or more of the following techniques:

- Probably the simplest and most effective option involves using non-trunk links in the core. By assigning each of these core links to a single VLAN (do *not* use VLAN 1 here!), the core will block the transmission of VLAN 1 information.

TIP	Consider using non-trunk links in the core. This can be an extremely simple but effective way to reduce "Sprawling VLANs" in your network.

- Use "switching routers" such as the Catalyst 8500s that do not forward VLAN 1 by default.
- Once it is available, use the upcoming feature that will allow VLAN 1 to be removed from trunk links (see the section "Deciding What Number Should be Used for the Management VLAN").
- If you are using an ATM core, VLAN 1 *can* be removed from this portion of the network (see Chapter 9 of *Cisco LAN Switching*).

NOTE	For the record, heavy broadcast traffic can also be a problem for routers. They are no different from other devices—all broadcasts must be processed to see if they are "interesting" or not. In fact, this phenomenon can be worse for routers because, by definition, they are connected to multiple subnets and therefore must process the broadcasts from every subnet.

However, with this being said, routers (and Layer 3 switches) are still the best tools for handling broadcast problems. Although the routers themselves can be susceptible to broadcast storms, their very use can greatly reduce the risk of Layer 2 loops ever forming. The multilayer model is designed to maximize this benefit by reducing Layer 2 connectivity to many small triangles and V's. Furthermore, although a broadcast loop can overload any directly-connected routers, the problem does not spread to other sections of the network, a huge improvement over the problems described earlier in this section and in the section "Use Separate Management VLANs."

Always Specify Your Root Bridges

Chapter 6 of *Cisco LAN Switching* discussed the problems that can arise when you do not manually specify Root Bridge locations in your network. It is highly possible (even probable if using older Cisco equipment) that a suboptimal bridge or switch wins the Root War election. Rather than leaving it to chance, always specify both a primary and a secondary Root Bridge for every VLAN (in a large and very flat network, it might be beneficial to also specify a tertiary Root Bridge). By manually setting the Root Bridges, it can not only optimize the data path, but it makes the network more deterministic and improves its stability, maintainability, and ease of troubleshooting.

TIP	All networks using groups of contiguous Layer 2 switches or transparent bridges should specify a primary and a backup Root Bridge.

Try to Use Root Bridge Placement Load Balancing

As discussed in Chapter 7 of *Cisco LAN Switching*, the Root Bridge placement form of Spanning Tree load balancing can be extremely effective and easy to implement if the topology supports it. In most networks that utilize campus-wide VLANs and a centralized server farm, it is very difficult to obtain any degree of load balancing with this technique.

However, when using the multilayer model in conjunction with MLS (and other types of routing switches), this form of load balancing is highly recommended. Because the multilayer model and MLS reduce the network to a series of many small Layer 2 triangles that span each IDF switch and the corresponding pair of MDF switches, the Layer 2 topology is constrained, well-defined, and deterministic. Consequently, it is easy to make one MDF switch the Root Bridge for approximately half of the VLANs contained in that distribution block while the other switch is configured as the Root Bridge for the remaining VLANs. (As a reminder, a distribution block is comprised of a pair of MDF switches and their associated collection of IDF switches—typically this is contained within a single building.) For example, Figure 3-9 illustrates a typical distribution block where MDF-A is the Root Bridge for the odd-numbered VLANs and MDF-B is the Root Bridge for the even-numbered VLANs.

Figure 3-9   *Root Bridge Placement Spanning Tree Load Balancing*

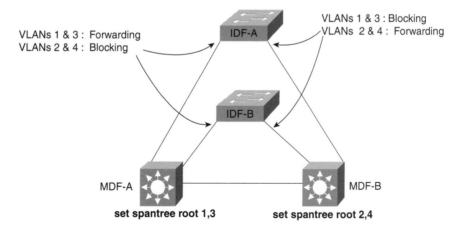

This causes the odd VLANs to use the left riser link (the right IDF port is Blocking for these VLANs), whereas the even VLANs use the right link (the left IDF port is Blocking). As discussed in the following section and Chapter 11 of *Cisco LAN Switching*, this should be coordinated with any Hot Standby Routing Protocol (HSRP) load balancing being performed by your MDF/distribution layer devices.

TIP   The Root Bridge placement form of Spanning Tree load balancing is both simple and effective.

Root Bridge Placement Considerations

Besides influencing traffic distribution through load balancing, several other factors should be considered when determining where Root Bridges should be located. Some of the more important considerations are mentioned in the following list:

- **Place the Root Bridge in the path of high-bandwidth data flows**—This point is discussed in more detail in the following section.

- **Use a device that is very stable**—Because Spanning Tree is a protocol that constantly seeks out the most attractive Root Bridge, placing the Root Bridge on a device that reboots or fails frequently can disturb the entire network unnecessarily.

- **Use a device that can carry the load**—Because the Root Bridge functions as a central switching node for all of the branches of the Spanning Tree, it must be able to handle the potentially high aggregate load.

When implementing a Spanning Tree design, most organizations adopt one of two strategies:

- Distributed Root Bridges
- Centralized Root Bridges

Distributed Root Bridge placement is useful in situations where network designers want to spread the centralized switching load over more than one bridge. Besides increasing the overall available bandwidth, this technique can also improve network stability by not forcing the entire network to depend on one or two switches for Root Bridge services. However, distributing the Root Bridges can significantly increase troubleshooting complexity in your network by creating a different logical topology for every VLAN.

TIP   In general, distributed Root Bridges can add more complexity to the network than they are worth.

Centralized Root Bridges are useful in situations where the traffic flows are highly concentrated (such as in the case of a centralized server farm). Another advantage of this approach is that it can ease troubleshooting by creating identical (or at least very similar) logical topologies in all VLANs. Overall, centralized Root Bridges are more common.

Where to Put Root Bridges

In general, the most important consideration is placing Root Bridges in the path of high-bandwidth data flows. The goal is to have the Spanning Tree logical topology mirror the natural flow of traffic in your network. To do otherwise implies an inefficient path for the most bandwidth-intensive flows. As discussed in Chapter 6 of *Cisco LAN Switching*, this optimization is most often achieved in one of two ways:

- When using very flat designs such as campus-wide VLANs, the Root Bridges should generally be placed at the point where the server farm connects to the campus core. Assuming that a pair of switches is used to link the server farm to the core (this provides redundancy as well as additional bandwidth), the Root Bridges can be alternated on a per-VLAN basis.

- When using routing switches (MLS) with the multilayer model, the Root Bridge should be located in the switch that contains (or, in the case of an external router, links to) the active HSRP peer for a given VLAN. Therefore, if an MDF switch is acting as the active HSRP peer for the odd-numbered VLANs, it should also be the primary Root Bridge for these VLANs.

Timer Tuning

Your decision to utilize Spanning Tree timer tuning should be based primarily on your campus architecture. If you have utilized the campus-wide VLAN model, timer tuning is almost always an exercise in futility and frustration. Because campus-wide VLANs lead to very large Spanning Tree domains, timer tuning usually results in a network plagued by instability.

TIP	Do not attempt Spanning Tree timer tuning if your network uses the campus-wide VLAN model.

On the other hand, the Layer 3 barriers created by the multilayer model make timer tuning a very attractive option for most networks. When performing timer tuning, it is usually best to use the **set spantree root** macro discussed in the "Using A Macro: **set spantree root**" section of Chapter 6 in *Cisco LAN Switching*. In general, the values in Table 3-1 have been shown to be a good compromise between network stability and speed of convergence (for more information on the details of these timer values, refer to Chapters 6 and 7 of *Cisco LAN Switching*).

Table 3-1 *Recommended Spanning Tree Timer Values*

Network Design	Specified Diameter	Specified Hello Time	Resulting Max Age	Resulting Forward Delay
Campus-wide VLANs	N/A	N/A	Default (20 secs)	Default (15 secs)
Multilayer and routing switches (MLS)	3 hops	2 secs	12 secs	9 secs
Multilayer and switching routers (8500s)	2 hops	2 secs	10 secs	7 secs

Because timer tuning is not recommended for campus-wide VLANs and should therefore not be specified on the **set spantree root** command, these values have been omitted from Table 3-1. (Although, as discussed in Chapter 7 of *Cisco LAN Switching*, 802.1D assumes a diameter of 7 hops and the Hello Time defaults to 2 seconds.) The routing switch (MLS) and switching router values are based on fairly conservative assumptions about link failures and the possibility of additional bridging devices being attached to the network (these values are also used and discussed in the case studies covered in Chapter 17 of *Cisco LAN Switching*).

Also, if you are willing and able to incur the extra load of Spanning Tree BPDUs, the Hello Time can be reduced to 1 second to further improve convergence times. However, notice that this doubles the bandwidth consumed by BPDUs, and, more importantly, the load on the supervisor CPUs. Therefore, if each device only participates in a small number of VLANs, Hello tuning can successfully improve Spanning Tree convergence times with minimal impact on the CPU. Conversely, if your devices participate in a large number of VLANs, changing the Hello Time can overload your CPUs. When using a large number of VLANs, only lower the Hello Time for a subset of the VLANs where you need the improved convergence time as a compromise. If lowering the Hello Time to one second, consider using the values specified in Table 3-2.

Table 3-2 *Spanning Tree Timer Values When Using a Hello Time of 1 Second*

Network Design	Specified Diameter	Specified Hello Time	Resulting Max Age	Resulting Forward Delay
Multilayer and routing switches (MLS)	3 hops	1 secs	7 secs	5 secs
Multilayer and switching routers (8500s)	2 hops	1 secs	5 secs	4 secs

Finally, be certain that you set the chosen timer values on both the primary and backup Root Bridges. You can set the values on other bridges/switches, but it has no effect (for simplicity, some organizations simply set the values on every device).

Spanning Tree and the Management VLAN

The point made earlier in the "Consider Using Loop-Free Management VLANs" section bears repeating—Layer 2 loops in the management VLAN can lead to catastrophic network failures. You should consider implementing loop-free VLANs for your management networks, especially if using a flat earth network topology.

Study Your Spanning Tree Logical Topology

The time to be learning your Spanning Tree logical topology is not during the middle of a major network outage. Instead, it is advisable to create maps of both your primary and backup Spanning Tree topologies beforehand. Most organizations are accustomed to making extensive use of diagrams that reveal the Layer 3 topology of their network (often using tools such as HP OpenView). However, very few of these same organizations go through the exercise of creating and distributing Layer 2 maps.

TIP	A picture is worth a thousand words... diagram your Layer 2 topologies (including Spanning Tree).

At a minimum, these diagrams should illustrate the extent of each VLAN, the location of the Root Bridge, and which switch-to-switch ports are Blocking or Forwarding (diagramming end-user ports is rarely beneficial). In addition, it might be useful to label the Forwarding ports as either Designated Ports or Root Ports. See Chapters 6 and 7 of *Cisco LAN Switching* for more information on these ports.

TIP	CiscoWorks 2000 can create basic Spanning Tree maps.

The importance of having Layer 2 diagrams is influenced by, once again, the choice of the network's design. They are especially important in the case of campus-wide VLANs where the combination of many VLANs and Blocking/Forwarding ports can become very complex. Fortunately, another benefit of the multilayer model is that it reduces the need for diagrams. First, the Layer 3 hierarchy created by this design makes the traditional Layer 3 maps much more useful. Second, the simplistic Layer 2 triangles and V's created by this design allow two or three template drawings to be used to document the entire Layer 2 network.

When to Use UplinkFast and BackboneFast

Both UplinkFast and BackboneFast are significant Cisco enhancements to the Spanning-Tree Protocol. It is important to know when and when not to use them. In general, neither feature is particularly useful in a network that contains a very strong Layer 3 switching component. Because this tends to break the network into a large number of loop-free paths, there are no Blocking ports for UplinkFast and BackboneFast to perform their magic.

TIP   Don't waste your time designing lots of Spanning Tree optimizations (such as UplinkFast and BackboneFast) into a heavily Layer 3-oriented network—they will have little or no effect.

On the other hand, UplinkFast and BackboneFast can be extremely useful in more Layer 2-oriented designs such as campus-wide VLANs and the multilayer model with routing switches (MLS). In either case, UplinkFast should be enabled only on IDF wiring closet switches while BackboneFast is enabled on every switch in each Spanning Tree domain. It is important to follow these guidelines. Although both protocols have been carefully engineered to not completely disable the network when they are used incorrectly, it causes the feature to either be completely ineffective (as is possible with BackboneFast) or to invalidate load balancing and Root Bridge placement (as is possible with UplinkFast). See Chapter 7 of *Cisco LAN Switching* for more detailed information on BackboneFast and UplinkFast.

When to Use PortFast

PortFast is a tool that deserves consideration in every network. There are two main benefits to using PortFast:

- End stations and some servers that use fault-tolerant NICs can gain immediate access to the network. In the case of end stations, this can help with protocols such as DHCP and initial server or directory authentication. For servers using fault-tolerant NICs that toggle link-state, PortFast can mean the difference between transparent failover and a 30–50 second outage (however, most fault-tolerant NICs do *not* toggle link). When using PortFast with server connections, be sure to disable PAgP on EtherChannel-capable ports. Otherwise PortFast still takes approximately 20 seconds to enable the link. For more information, please refer to the section "Disabling Port Aggregation Protocol" in Chapter 7 of *Cisco LAN Switching*.

- Ports do not send Topology Change Notification (TCN) BPDUs when they are using PortFast. Because TCNs cause bridges and switches to use a shorter bridge aging period, an excess of these packets can destabilize a large campus network (especially with flat earth designs like campus-wide VLANs). By potentially eliminating tens of thousands of TCNs per day in the typical large campus network, the use of PortFast can have a significant impact.

Even though Catalysts allow you to enter the **set spantree portfast** *mod_num/port_num* **enable** command on a trunk link, the command is ignored. Despite this feature, it is best to leave PortFast disabled on trunk links and spare other administrators of the network some confusion when they see it enabled.

TIP	Although PortFast is extremely useful in Ethernet-only networks, you might wish to avoid its use in networks that employ a LANE core. Because PortFast suppresses TCN BPDUs, it can interfere with LANE's process of learning about devices/MAC addresses that have been relocated to a different LANE-attached switch. As a result, nodes that relocate may have to wait five minutes (by default) for their connectivity to be re-established if PortFast is in use.
	By disabling PortFast, LANE will receive a TCN (both when the node is initially disconnected from the original switch *and* when it is reconnected to the new switch) that shortens the MAC aging process to the Spanning Tree Forward Delay timer (see Chapter 6 of *Cisco LAN Switching*). As an alternative you can manually (and permanently) lower the bridge table aging period using the **set cam agingtime** command. Both techniques will cause LANE to remove the MAC address to NSAP address mapping in the LES more quickly and force it to relearn the new mapping for a device that has been relocated. See Chapter 7 of *Cisco LAN Switching* for more detailed information on the operation of LANE.

When One Spanning Tree Is Not Enough

Although many people complain that one Spanning Tree per VLAN is too complex for human comprehension (by the way, this is an exaggeration), there are times when you actually want to use more than one Spanning Tree per VLAN! Other than the corner-case of using PVST+ to tunnel multiple Spanning Trees through an 802.1Q region that only utilizes a single Spanning Tree, the primary use of multiple Spanning Trees per VLAN is to successfully integrate bridging and routing between VLANs. (See the "Per-VLAN Spanning Tree Plus" section of Chapter 7 in *Cisco LAN Switching* for more information on PVST+). When combining bridging and routing, the situation can arise where IP subnets become partitioned and a partial loss of connectivity occurs—for example, when bridging protocols such as NetBIOS and LAT while simultaneously routing traffic such as IP. Chapter 11 of *Cisco LAN Switching* referred to this as the broken subnet problem in the "Issues and Caveats with Bridging between VLANS" section and the "How to Fix the Broken Subnet Problem" section.

TIP	Watch out for the "broken subnet problem." It can create difficult to troubleshoot connectivity problems.

As detailed in Chapter 11 of *Cisco LAN Switching*, the solution is to use two versions of the Spanning-Tree Protocol. The Layer 2 Catalysts such as the 5000 and the 6000 only use the IEEE version of the Spanning-Tree Protocol. However, IOS-based devices such as the routers and Catalyst 8500s can either run the DEC version of Spanning Tree-Protocol or Cisco's proprietary VLAN-Bridge Spanning-Tree Protocol. In both cases, the BPDUs for these two protocols are treated as normal multicast data by the Layer 2 Catalysts and flooded normally. Conversely, the IOS-based devices swallow the IEEE BPDUs when they are running a different version of the Spanning-Tree Protocol. Consequently, the IOS-based devices partition the IEEE protocol into smaller pockets. Within each pocket, the IEEE Spanning-Tree Protocol ensures that the logical topology is loop free. The DEC or VLAN-Bridge version of the Spanning-Tree Protocol ensures that the collection of pockets remains loop free. The result is a network where both routed and non-routed protocols have full connectivity throughout the network. For more information, see the "Using Different Spanning-Tree Protocols" section in Chapter 11 of *Cisco LAN Switching*.

Load Balancing

Load balancing can be one of the telltale signs that indicate whether a network has been carefully planned or if it has grown up like weeds. By allowing redundant links to effectively double the available bandwidth, load balancing is something that every network should strive to implement.

This chapter briefly mentions the most popular alternatives available for implementing load balancing. As you go through this section, recognize that none of these accomplish round robin or per-packet load balancing. Therefore, although these techniques are most often referred to with the name load balancing, the name load sharing or load distribution might be more appropriate. However, do not get hung up with trying to achieve an exact 50/50 split when you implement load balancing over a pair of links. Just remember that any form of load balancing is preferable to the default operation of most campus protocols where only a single path is ever used.

Remember the Requirements for Load Balancing

Before diving into the details of various approaches to load balancing, it is worth pausing to examine some high-level considerations of load balancing. When thinking about load balancing, first look at the number of available paths. If you have only one set of paths through your network, load balancing (and, therefore, redundancy) is not possible. Most network designers strive to achieve two paths, as typically seen connected to an IDF/access layer switch. In some cases, especially inside a large campus core, more than two paths might be available.

Another consideration is the ease with which you can configure, manage, and troubleshoot a particular load balancing scheme. For example, the Root Bridge placement form of Spanning Tree load balancing is very easy to implement and troubleshoot.

Also, look at the flexibility of each style of load balancing. For instance, although Root Bridge placement scores very high on the simplicity scale, it can only be implemented in selected topologies (such as the Layer 2 triangles used by the multilayer model). By way of contrast, the **portvlancost** method of Spanning Tree load balancing is very flexible (however, it is also more complex).

Finally, consider the intelligence of a load balancing scheme. For example, some techniques such as EtherChannel use a very simple **XOR** algorithm on the low-order bits of IP or MAC address. On the other hand, Layer 3 routing protocols offer very sophisticated and tunable load balancing and, more importantly, path selection tools.

TIP   Important load balancing considerations include:

- Available paths

- Ease of configuration, management, and troubleshooting

- Flexibility

- Intelligence

Spanning Tree

Spanning Tree load balancing is useful within a redundant Layer 2 domain. As discussed in Chapter 7 of *Cisco LAN Switching*, there are four techniques available for load balancing under the Spanning-Tree Protocol:

- Root Bridge placement

- Port priority (**portvlanpri**)

- Bridge priority

- Port cost (**portvlancost**)

As discussed in Chapter 7 of *Cisco LAN Switching* and earlier in this chapter, Root Bridge placement is the simplest and most effective technique if the network's traffic flows support it. Fortunately, the multilayer model with routing switches (MLS) automatically generates a topology where the Root Bridges can be alternated between redundant MDF switches within a distribution block.

TIP   When working with the Spanning-Tree Protocol, try not to use the Root Bridge placement form of Spanning Tree load balancing.

Root Bridge placement is not effective in less constrained topologies such as campus-wide VLANs. In these cases, it is best to use the **portvlancost** form of load balancing. Although **portvlancost** is harder to use than Root Bridge placement, it is useful in almost any redundant topology. Think of it as the Swiss army knife of Spanning Tree load balancing.

TIP   When working with the Spanning-Tree Protocol, use **portvlancost** load balancing when the use of Root Bridge placement is not possible.

HSRP

In situations where Layer 3 switching is being used, HSRP plays an important role. When using Layer 3 switching in networks that contain Layer 2 loops in the distribution block, such as with the multilayer model and routing switches (MLS), Spanning Tree and HSRP load balancing should be deployed in a coordinated fashion. For example, the network in Figure 3-9 modified the Spanning Tree parameters to force the odd VLANs to use the left link and the even VLANs to use the right link. HSRP should be added to this design by making MDF-A the active HSRP peer for the odd VLANs and MDF-B the active peer for the even VLANs.

TIP

Be sure to coordinate HSRP and Spanning Tree load balancing. This is usually required in networks employing routing switches and the multilayer model.

In cases where the switching router (8500) approach to the multilayer model is in use, HSRP might be the only option available for load balancing within each distribution block (there are no loops for Spanning Tree to be effective). Consequently, two HSRP groups should be used for each subnet. This configuration was discussed in Chapter 11 of *Cisco LAN Switching* and is referred to as Multigroup HSRP (MHSRP). MHSRP can be used to load balance by alternating the HSRP priority values.

TIP

Use MHSRP load balancing for networks using switching router technology.

Figure 3-10 illustrates an example that provides load balancing for one subnet/VLAN on an IDF switch.

Figure 3-10   *MHSRP Load Balancing*

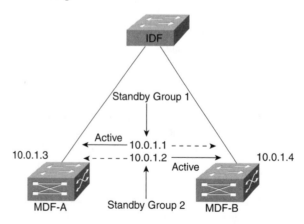

Both of the MDF switches are assigned two real IP addresses, 10.0.1.3 and 10.0.1.4. Rather than using a single standby group (which results in only one router and one riser link actively carrying traffic), two standby groups are configured. The first standby group uses an IP address of 10.0.1.1 and the priority of MDF-A has been increased to make it the active peer. The second standby group uses 10.0.1.2 and has MDF-B configured as the active peer. If both MDF switches are active, both riser links and both devices actively carry traffic. If either MDF device fails, the other MDF takes over with 100 percent of the load.

IP Routing

Another advantage in using Layer 3 switching is that IP routing protocols support very intelligent forwarding and path determination mechanisms. Whereas it can take considerable configuration to enable load balancing over two paths using techniques such as Spanning Tree load balancing and HSRP, Cisco routers automatically load balance up to six equal-cost paths (although Catalyst 8500s currently only load balance over two equal-cost paths because of the microcode memory limitations). Moreover, Layer 3 routing protocols support extensive path manipulation tools such as distribute lists and route maps.

Given that the multilayer design model focuses on Layer 3 switching in the MDF/distribution layer closets (and possibly the core), IP routing can be an extremely effective approach to load balancing across critical areas of the network such as the core (expensive WAN links are another area).

ATM

One of the benefits in using ATM in a campus environment is the sophistication of Private Network-Network Interface (PNNI) as an ATM routing and signaling protocol. Like IP, PNNI automatically load balances traffic over multiple paths. However, unlike IP, PNNI does not perform routing on every unit of information that it receives (cells). Instead, ATM only routes the initial call setup that is used to build the ATM connection. After the connection has been established, all remaining cells follow this single path. However, other calls between the same two ATM switches can use a different set of paths through a redundant ATM network (therefore, PNNI is said to do per connection load balancing). In this way, all of the paths within the ATM cloud are automatically utilized.

For more information on ATM, LANE, and PNNI, please consult Chapter 9, "Trunking with LAN Emulation," of *Cisco LAN Switching*.

EtherChannel

A final form of load balancing that can be useful for campus networks is EtherChannel. EtherChannel can only be used between a pair of back-to-back switches connected between two and eight links (although some platforms allow limited combinations). It uses an XOR algorithm on the low-order bits of MAC or IP addresses to assign frames to individual links. For more information, see Chapter 8, "Trunking Technologies and Applications," of *Cisco LAN Switching*

| TIP | The 802.3ad committee of the IEEE is working on a standards-based protocol similar to Cisco's EtherChannel. |

Routing/Layer 3 Switching

As this chapter has already mentioned many times, Layer 3 switching is a key ingredient in most successful large campus networks. This section elaborates on some issues specific to Layer 3 switching.

Strive for Modularity

One of the primary benefits of using Layer 3 technology is that it can create a high degree of modularity in a design. For instance, Figure 3-11 illustrates a typical two-building campus using the multilayer model.

Figure 3-11 *Using a Layer 3 Barrier to Create a Modular Design*

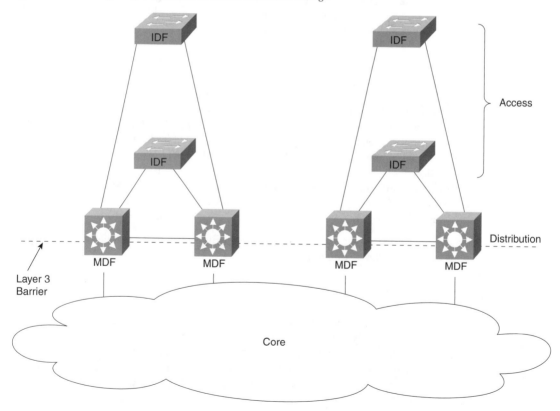

The Layer 3 barrier created by the routing function embedded in the MDF switches separates each building from the core. The primary benefits of this technique are:

- The modularity allows for cookie-cutter designs. Although the IP addresses (as well as other Layer 3 protocol addresses) change, each distribution block can be implemented with almost identical switch and router code.

- The network is very easy to understand and troubleshoot. Technicians can apply most of the same skills used for managing and troubleshooting router and hub networks.

- The network is highly scalable. As new buildings or server farms are added to the campus, they merely become new distribution blocks off the core.

- The network is very deterministic. As devices or links fail, the traffic will failover in clearly defined ways.

Although some degree of modularity can be created with more Layer 2-oriented designs such as campus-wide VLANs, it is much more difficult to get the separation required for true modularity. Without a Layer 3 barrier of scalability, the Layer 2 protocols tend to become intertwined and tightly coupled. Consequently, it becomes more difficult to grow and rearrange the network.

When to Use MLS (and Routing Switches)

The routing switch (MLS) form of the multilayer model is most appropriate when you want to maintain a strong Layer 2 component within each distribution block. By doing so, MLS allows the feature-rich Layer 2 Catalysts to flourish. Options such as VTP and PVST can all be very useful in this environment. Also, by maintaining this strong Layer 2 orientation, you can easily place a single VLAN on multiple IDF/access layer wiring closets (8500s require bridging/IRB to accomplish this). Furthermore, MLS has excellent support for multiprotocol routing, as well as combining routing and bridging within the same device. For more information on the specific benefits and configuration commands for MLS, see Chapter 11, Chapter 14, and Chapter 17 of *Cisco LAN Switching*.

When to Use Switching Routers (8500s)

Whereas MLS maintains a Layer 2 flavor within the distribution block, switching routers go to the opposite extreme. Switching routers such as the Catalyst 8540 are most easily configured and maintained when functioning as a pure router. Although they do support bridging through the use of IRB and bridge groups, extensive use of these features can lead to configurations that are difficult to maintain.

Instead, by using these devices as very high-speed routers, they can dramatically simplify network design. Issues and problems associated with Spanning Tree all but disappear. Traffic flows become highly deterministic. Support personnel accustomed to working in the traditional router and hub model find switching router designs easy to support and troubleshoot. The superior support of IP multicast technology at Layer 3 provides an excellent migration path to the future.

As with MLS, more information can be found on the pros and cons of switching routers in Chapters 11, 14, and 17 of *Cisco LAN Switching*.

When to Use IRB

In short, use IRB only when you have to. It is not that IRB is a bad feature. In fact, IRB is a very flexible technology for combining Layer 2 and Layer 3 traffic and it allows precise control over how both bridged and routed traffic is handled. The problem is more likely to be a human one—IRB can be difficult to understand, support, and design.

When considering the use of IRB, also take into account the following issues:

- An advantage to doing IRB on hardware-based platforms such as the Catalyst 8500 is that it can be performed at wire speed (the software-based routers are currently limited to fast-switching speeds).

- There is a limit to the number of Bridged Virtual Interfaces (BVIs) that the IOS supports (currently 64).

- Some features are not supported on BVIs. Because the list is constantly changing, check the release notes or place a call to Cisco's TAC.

When deciding where to utilize IRB, try to use it only as a tool for specific niche issues— for example, if you need to place several directly-connected servers into a single VLAN or if there is a VLAN that absolutely must transit a switching router.

TIP

If your design calls for the extensive use of IRB, consider using the Catalyst 6000 "Native IOS Mode" detailed in Chapter 18 of *Cisco LAN Switching*. In general, it will result in a network that is considerably easier to configure and maintain.

Limit Unnecessary Router Peering

When using routers in VLAN-based networks, it can be important to reduce unnecessary router peering. For example, consider cases such as those illustrated in Figure 3-7 and Figure 3-10. Assume that these routers connect to 30 wiring closet VLANs via ISL or 802.1Q trunks. By default, the routers will form 30 separate adjacencies, wasting valuable router memory and processor power. By listing all or most of these VLANs as passive interfaces for the routing protocol, this can dramatically reduce this unnecessary peering. For wiring closet VLANs where no other routers are located, all VLANs should be removed.

TIP

Reducing unnecessary peering can be especially important with Catalyst 8500 routers and the Catalyst 6000 MSM.

Load Balancing

As discussed in the Spanning Tree sections, the style of load balancing that is needed depends primarily on the type of Layer 3 switching that is in use. To summarize the earlier discussion, MLS generally requires that a combination of Spanning Tree and HSRP load balancing techniques be used within the distribution block. When using switching routers, MHSRP should be used.

Also, Layer 3 switches automatically load balance across the campus core if equal-cost paths are available.

Try to Use Only Routable Protocols

Unless it is absolutely necessary, try to pass only routable protocols through your Layer 3 switches. This is most often accomplished by relegating non-routable protocols to a single VLAN. If you are migrating to a new network infrastructure, consider leaving the non-routable traffic on the old infrastructure. The lagging performance of that network serves as an incentive for users of non-routable protocols to upgrade to an IP-based application.

ATM

As Layer 3 switching has grown in popularity, it has demonstrated that ATM is not the only technology capable of great speed. However, ATM does have its place in many campus networks. This section examines some of the more important issues associated with completing an ATM-based campus network design.

When to Use ATM

One of the first questions every network designer must face is should the design utilize ATM technology. In the past, ATM has been billed as the solution to every possible network problem. Although this might be true in terms of ATM's theoretical capabilities, it is not true in terms of how most organizations are using ATM. For example, in the mid-1990s, many network analysts foretold of the coming days where networks would use ATM on an end-to-end basis. Instead, Ethernet has continued to grow in popularity. When, then, is it best to use cell-based switching?

Traditionally, ATM has been touted for several unique benefits. The most commonly mentioned benefits include:

- **High bandwidth**—Because cells use fixed-size units of data with simple and predictable header formats, it is fairly easy to create high-speed hardware-based switching equipment.

- **Sophisticated bandwidth sharing**—Cells can be interleaved to allow multiple communication sessions to share a single link through an advanced form of statistical multiplexing. Because cells are all the same size, applications using large data transfer units do not create a log jam effect that slows down smaller and potentially more time-sensitive traffic.

- **Quality of Service (QoS)**—ATM has complex and sophisticated mechanisms to allow detailed traffic contracts to be specified and enforced.

- **Support for voice and video**—ATM's low latency and QoS benefit give it robust support for time-critical forms of communication such as voice and video.

- **Distance**—Unlike common campus technologies such as Ethernet, ATM can function over any distance.

- **Interoperability**—Because ATM is a global standard, a wide variety of devices can be purchased from different vendors.

Although many of these points remain true, advances in frame-based switching have significantly eroded ATMs edge in the following areas:

- Campus-oriented Gigabit Ethernet switches now match or exceed the speed of ATM switches. Although cell switching does maintain a theoretical advantage, ASIC-based Layer 2 and Layer 3 switches have become exceptionally fast. Furthermore, ATM has continued to struggle with the SAR boundary, the fastest speed that ATM's Segmentation And Reassembly function can be performed.

- Ethernet-based QoS (or at least Class of Service) schemes are becoming more available, more practical, and more effective. Although ATM holds a theoretical lead, ATM continues to suffer from a lack of applications that capitalize on its inherently superior capabilities. As a result, CoS-capable Gigabit Ethernet switches are rapidly growing in popularity.

- Although ATM does maintain a distinct advantage in its capability to handle isochronous (timing critical) applications, there is tremendous growth in non-isochronous mechanisms for sending voice and video traffic. Efforts such as voice over IP (VoIP) and H.323 videoconferencing are common examples. These technologies reduce the need for ATM's unique capabilities.

- Gigabit Ethernet distances are growing dramatically. As this book goes to press, a number of vendors are introducing 80–100 km Gigabit Ethernet products.

- All forms of Ethernet, including Gigabit Ethernet, have been perceived as being considerably more interoperable than ATM standards.

In addition, the complexity of ATM has become a significant issue for most organizations. Whereas Ethernet is considered easy and familiar, ATM is considered difficult and murky (and, to a significant extent, these perceptions are valid).

TIP

Although the growth of ATM in campus networks has slowed at the time this book goes to press, it is important to note that the use of ATM technology in the WAN continues to expand rapidly.

Where to Use ATM

Although there is considerable debate about the usefulness of ATM in a campus backbone, there is considerably less debate about where it is useful. Almost all analysts are in agreement that desktop connections will be Ethernet for the foreseeable future. Although 10/100 Ethernet sales continue to soar, sales of ATM to the desktop have staggered. When ATM is used, almost all agree that the ATM is best suited to the core of the network. In most cases, this means a LANE core connecting to Ethernet switches containing LANE uplink modules.

Although this issue has received fairly little debate, a second issue has been less clear-cut. The issue concerns the matter of how far the ATM backbone should reach. The debate surrounds two options.

Some vendors and network designers prefer to link only the MDF/distribution layer devices to the ATM core. Fast and Gigabit Ethernet links can then be used to connect to IDF switches as shown in Figure 3-12.

Figure 3-12   *Using Ethernet Links in Conjunction with an ATM Core*

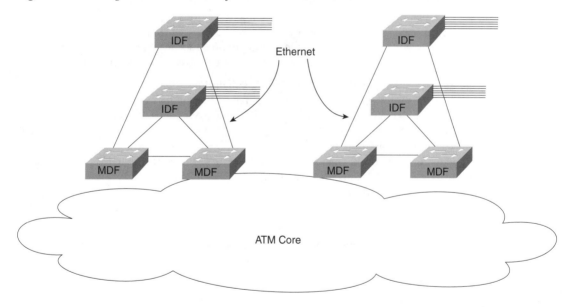

The advantage of this approach is that it uses cost-effective Ethernet technology in the potentially large number of IDF closets. This design is often deployed using the campus-wide VLAN model to extend the speed of ATM through the Ethernet links. The downside is that it creates a large number of Layer 2 loops where redundant MDF-to-IDF links are used. Unfortunately, these links have been shown to create Spanning Tree loops that can disable the entire campus network. Furthermore, it is harder to use ATM features such as QoS when the edges of the network use Ethernet.

The opposing view is that the ATM backbone should extend all the way to the IDF closets. Under this design, the entire network utilizes ATM except for the links that directly connect to end-user devices. This approach is illustrated in Figure 3-13.

Figure 3-13   *Extending the ATM Core to the IDF Switches*

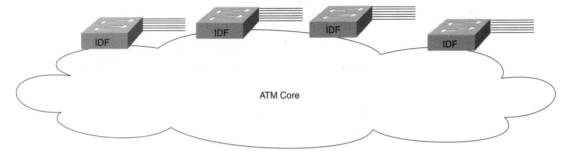

The downside of this alternative is a potentially higher cost because it requires more ATM uplink and switch ports. However, the major benefit of this design is that it eliminates the Layer 2 loops formed by the Ethernet links in the previous approach. Because LANE inherently creates a loop-free Layer 2 topology, the risk of Spanning Tree problems is considerably less (in fact, some vendors who promote this design leave Spanning Tree disabled by default, something many network engineers feel is a risky move).

Having worked with implementations using both designs, I feel that the answer should be driven by the use of Layer 3 switching (like many other things). If you are using the multilayer model to create hard Layer 3 barriers in the MDF/distribution layer devices, the MDF switches can be the attachment point to the ATM core and Ethernet links to the IDF devices can be safely used. However, when the campus-wide VLAN model is in use, extending the ATM backbone to the IDFs allows for the most stable and scalable design. Trying to use the MDF-attachment method with campus-wide VLANs results in Spanning Tree loops and network stability issues.

TIP   The use of Layer 3 switching in your network should drive the design of an ATM core.

Using SSRP

Until standards-based LANE redundancy mechanisms become widely available, Simple Server Redundancy Protocol (SSRP) will remain an important feature in almost any LANE-based core using Cisco ATM switches. Although SSRP allows more than one set of redundant devices, experience has shown that this can lead to scaling problems. See Chapter 9 of *Cisco LAN Switching* for more information on SSRP.

BUS Placement

Always try to place your LANE Broadcast and Unknown Server (BUS) on a Catalyst LANE module. Because the BUS must handle every broadcast and multicast packet in the ELAN (at least in current versions of the protocols), the potential traffic volume can be extremely high. The Catalyst 5000 OC-3 and Catalyst 5000/6000 OC-12 LANE modules offer approximately 130 kpps and 450 kpps of BUS performance respectively, considerably more than any other Cisco device currently offered.

One decision faced by designers of large LANE cores involves whether a single BUS or multiple distributed BUSes should be utilized. The advantage of a single BUS is that every ELAN has the same logical topology (at least the primary topologies are the same, the backup SSRP topology is obviously different). The disadvantage is that the single BUS can more easily become a bottleneck.

Distributed BUSes allow each ELAN to have a different BUS. Although this can offer significantly higher aggregate BUS throughput, it can make the network harder to manage and troubleshoot. With the introduction of OC-12 LANE modules and their extremely high BUS performance, it is generally advisable to use a single BUS and capitalize on the simplicity of having a single logical topology for every ELAN.

TIP   With the high BUS throughput available with modern equipment, centralized BUS designs are most common today.

Chapter 9 of *Cisco LAN Switching* contains additional information on BUS placement.

MPOA

Multiprotocol Over ATM (MPOA) can be a useful technology for improving Layer 3 performance. MPOA, as discussed in Chapter 10, "Trunking with Multiprotocol over ATM," of *Cisco LAN Switching* allows shortcut virtual circuits to be created and avoids the use of routers for extended flows. When considering the use of MPOA, keep the following points in mind:

- MPOA can only create shortcuts in sections of the network that use ATM. Therefore, if the MDF devices attach to an ATM core but Ethernet is used to connect from the MDF to the IDF switches, MPOA is only useful within the core itself. If the core does not contain Layer 3 hops, MPOA offers no advantage over LANE. In general, MPOA is most useful when the ATM cloud extends to the IDF/access layer switches.

- Because MPOA is mainly designed for networks using ATM on an IDF-to-IDF basis, you must intentionally build Layer 3 barriers into the network. Without careful planning, MPOA can lead to flat earth networks and the associated scaling problems discussed earlier in this chapter and in Chapters 11, 14, and 17 of *Cisco LAN Switching*.

- At presstime, significant questions remain about the stability and scalability of MPOA.

TIP	MPOA only optimizes unicast traffic (however, related protocols such as a MARS can be used to improve multicast performance).

Hardware Changes

In most Catalyst equipment (such as the Catalyst 5000), both MPOA and LANE use MAC addresses from the chassis or Supervisor to automatically generate ATM NSAP addresses. For a detailed discussion of how NSAP addresses are created, refer to Chapter 9 of *Cisco LAN Switching*. When designing an ATM network, keep the following address-related points in mind:

- Devices with active backplanes such as the Catalyst 5500s use MAC addresses pulled from the backplane itself. Changing the chassis of one of these devices therefore changes the automatically-generated NSAP addresses.

- Devices with passive backplanes such as the Catalyst 5000 use MAC addresses from the Supervisor. Therefore, changing a Catalyst 5000 Supervisor module changes the pool of addresses used for automatically generating NSAP addresses.

- In both cases, 16 MAC addresses are assigned to each slot. Therefore, simply moving a LANE module to a different slot alters the automatically generated NSAP addresses.

- Because of these concerns, many organizations prefer to use hard-coded NSAP addresses. For more information, see the section "Using Hard-Coded Addresses" in Chapter 9 of *Cisco LAN Switching*.

TIP	Consider using hard-coded NSAP addresses in a large LANE network.

Campus Migrations

It can be very challenging to manage a campus migration. New devices are brought online as older equipment is decommissioned or redeployed. However, while the rollout is taking place, connectivity must be maintained between the two portions of the network. This section makes a few high-level recommendations.

Use the Overlay Approach

During a migration, many organizations attempt to intermingle old and new equipment on the same links to form a single network. Although this does appear appealing from the perspective of trying to maintain full connectivity during the migration, it can make the rollout extremely difficult. By intermingling the two sets of equipment, the new network can be dragged down by the old equipment. Problems such as excessive bridging for non-routable protocols and Spanning Tree issues can prevent the new network from living up to its full potential. Moreover, if two Gigabit-speed switches are forced to communicate through an existing software-based router, it is like trying to drive a 6000 hp dragster down a dirt road!

In general, the most effective solution for dealing with campus migrations is to use the overlay technique.

As shown in Figure 3-14, the overlay approach treats the two networks as totally separate. Rather than connecting the new devices to the existing links, a completely out-of-band set of new links are used. If old and new devices are located in the same wiring closet, both connect to separate links. Therefore, the new network is said to overlay the existing network.

Figure 3-14   *The Overlay Approach to Campus Migrations*

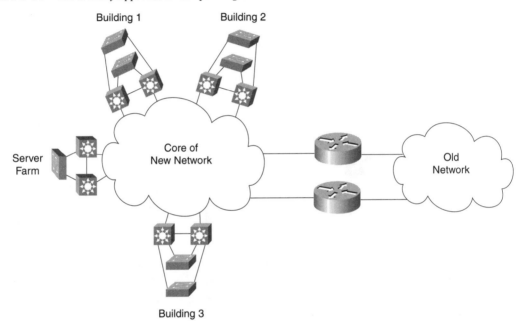

To maintain connectivity between the old and the new network, a pair of redundant routers is used. This provides a single line where the two networks meet. Issues such as route redistribution and access lists can be easily handled here. Also notice that this causes the old network to resemble just another distribution block connected to the core of the new network (another benefit of the modularity created by the multilayer model).

Server Farms

Servers play a critical role in modern networks. Given this importance, they should be considered early in the design process. This section discusses some common issues associated with server farm design.

Where to Place Servers

Most organizations are moving toward centralized server farms to allow better support and management of the servers themselves. Given this trend, it is generally best to position a centralized server farm as another distribution block attached to the campus core. This concept is illustrated in Figure 3-15.

Figure 3-15 *Centralized Server Farm*

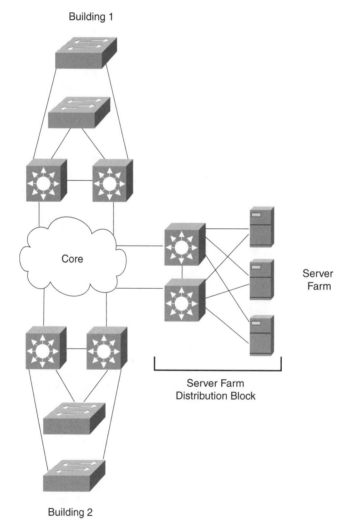

The servers in Figure 3-15 can be connected by a variety of means. The figure shows the servers directly connected to the pair of Layer 3 switches that link to the campus core. An alternative design is to use one or more Layer 2 switches within the server farm. These Layer 2 devices can then be connected to the Layer 3 switches through Gigabit Ethernet or Gigabit EtherChannel. Although some servers can connect to only a single switch, redundant NICs provide a measure of fault-tolerance.

The key to this design is the Layer 3 barrier created by the pair of Layer 3 switches that link the server farm to the core. Not only does this insulate the server farm from the core, but it also creates a much more modular design.

Some network designs directly connect the servers to the core as shown in Figure 3-16.

Figure 3-16   *Connecting Servers Directly to the Campus Core*

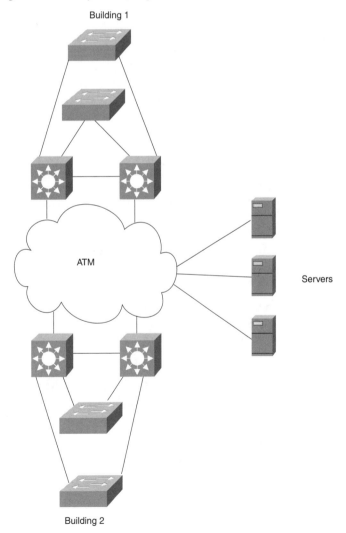

Figure 3-16 illustrates a popular method used for core-attached servers—using an ATM core. By installing LANE-capable ATM NICs in the servers, the servers can directly join the ELAN used in the campus core. A similar design could have been built using ISL or 802.1Q NICs in the servers.

Most organizations run into one of two problems when using servers directly connected to the campus core:

- Inefficient flows
- Poor performance

The first problem occurs with implementations of the multilayer model where the routing component contained in the MDF/distribution layer devices can lead to inefficient flows. For example, consider Figure 3-16. Assume that one of the servers needs to communicate with an end user in Building 1. When using default gateway technology, the server does not know which MDF Layer 3 switch to send the packets to. Some form of Layer 3 knowledge is required as packets leave the server farm. One way to achieve this is to run a routing protocol on the servers themselves. However, this can limit your choice of routing protocols throughout the remainder of the network, and many server administrators are reluctant to configure routing protocols on their servers. A cleaner approach is to simply position the entire server farm behind a pair of Layer 3 switches, as shown in Figure 3-15.

The second problem occurs with implementations of campus-wide VLANs where the servers can be made to participate in every VLAN used throughout the campus (for example, most LANE NICs allow multiple ELANs to be configured). Although this sounds extremely attractive on paper (it can eliminate most of the need for routers in the campus), these multi-VLAN NICs often have poor performance and are subject to frequent episodes of strange behavior (for example, browsing services in a Microsoft-based network). Moreover, this approach suffers from all of the scalability concerns discussed earlier in this chapter and in Chapters 14 and 17 of *Cisco LAN Switching*.

In general, it is best to always place a centralized server farm behind Layer 3 switches. Not only does this provide intelligent forwarding to the MDF switches located throughout the rest of the campus, but it also provides a variety of other benefits:

- This placement encourages fast convergence.
- Access lists can be configured on the Layer 3 switches to secure the server farm.
- Server-to-server traffic is kept off of the campus core. This can not only improve performance, but it can also improve security.
- It is highly scalable.
- Layer 3 switches have excellent multicast support, an important consideration for campuses making widespread use of multicast technology.

Consider Distributed Server Farms

Although centralized server farms are becoming increasingly common because they simplify server management, they do create problems from a bandwidth management perspective because the aggregate data rate can be extremely high. Although high-speed Layer 2 and Layer 3 switches have mitigated this problem to a certain extent, network designers should look for opportunities to intelligently distribute servers throughout the organization. Although this point is obviously true with regards to wide-area links, it can also be true of campus networks.

One occasion where servers can fairly easily be distributed is in the case of departmental servers (servers that are dedicated to a single organizational unit). These devices can be directly connected to the distribution block network they serve. In general, these servers are attached in one of two locations:

- They can be directly connected to the IDF switch that handles the given department.
- They can be attached to the MDF switches in that building or distribution block. This also presents the opportunity to create mini server farms in the MDF closets of every building. Departmental file and print servers can be attached here where enterprise and high-maintenance servers can be located in the centralized server farm.

Use Fault-Tolerant NICs

Many organizations spend numerous hours and millions of dollars creating highly redundant campus networks. However, much of this money and effort can go to waste unless the servers themselves are also redundant. A fairly simple way to improve a server's redundancy is to install some sort of redundant NICs.

Although using redundant NICs can be as simple as just installing two normal NICs in each server, this approach can lead to problems in the long run. Because most network operating systems require each of these NICs to use different addresses, clients need some mechanism to failover to the address assigned to the secondary NIC when the primary fails. This can be challenging to implement.

Instead, it is advisable to use special NICs that automatically support failover using a single MAC and Layer 3 address. In this case, the failover can be completely transparent to the end stations. A variety of these fault-tolerant NICs are available (some also support multiple modes of fault tolerance, allowing customization of network performance).

TIP	Fault-tolerant NICs allow two (or more) server NICs to share a single Layer 2 and Layer 3 address.

When selecting a fault-tolerant NIC, also consider what sort of load balancing it supports (some do no load balancing, and others only load balance in one direction). Finally, closely analyze the technique used by the NICs to inform the rest of the network that a change has occurred. For example, many NICs perform a gratuitous ARP to force an update in neighboring switches.

In some cases, this update process can be fairly complex and require a compromise of timer values. For example, when using fault-tolerant Ethernet NICs in conjunction with a LANE backbone, it is not enough to simply update the Layer 2 CAM tables and Layer 3 ARP tables. If redundant LANE modules are used to access the server farm, the LANE LE-ARP tables (containing MAC address to ATM NSAP address mappings) also need to be updated. When faced with this issue, you might be forced to disable PortFast and intentionally incur a Spanning Tree delay. The upside of this delay is that it triggers a LANE topology change message and forces the LE-ARP tables to update.

Obviously, redundant NICs should be carefully planned and thoroughly tested *before* a real network outage occurs.

TIP   You may need to disable PAgP on server ports using fault-tolerant NICs to support the binding protocols used by some of these NICs during initialization.

Use Secured VLANs in Server Farms

Cisco is developing a new model for VLANs to provide simple but effective security for applications such as very large server farms. Under this feature, one or more uplink ports are configured on each of the switches used to directly link the servers to one or more default gateways. These ports support two-way access to all servers within the VLAN. However, other ports within the VLAN designated as access or server ports cannot communicate with each other. This creates an easy-to-administer environment where the servers have full communication with the network's backbone/core but with no risk of the servers communicating with each other. This feature will be extremely useful in situations such as Internet service provider (ISP) web hosting facilities where communication between servers from different clients must be tightly controlled. Whereas earlier solutions generally involved creating hundreds of small VLANs and IP subnets, Cisco's new model of VLAN will be much easier to implement and maintain (all of the servers can use a single VLAN and IP subnet) while providing tight security.

NOTE   This feature had not received an official name at the time this book goes to press. Contact your Cisco sales team for additional information.

Additional Campus Design Recommendations

This section addresses a variety of other tips and best practices that do not fit in the previous sections or important points that deserve emphasis.

Access Layer Recommendations

When designing the IDF/access layer sections of the network, be sure to at least consider using the following features if NFFC/RSFC support is available in these devices:

- Protocol Filtering (see Chapter 11 of *Cisco LAN Switching*)
- IGMP Snooping (see Chapter 12 of *Cisco LAN Switching*)
- QoS classification

Distribution Layer Recommendations

The recommendation here is simple and has been clearly discussed earlier in the chapter. However, it is important enough to repeat: *Always try to form a Layer 3 barrier in the MDF/distribution layer devices.*

Core Layer Recommendations

The primary thing to keep in mind is the point discussed in the Spanning Tree and VLAN sections: *Keep the core loop free when using a Layer 2 core.*

Watch Out for Discontiguous Subnets

Carefully scrutinize your designs for possible discontiguous subnets. One of the most common and subtle causes of this situation is created in scenarios such as that shown in Figure 3-17.

Figure 3-17   *Discontiguous Subnets*

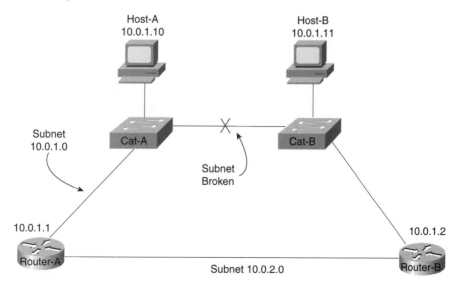

The link between Cat-A and Cat-B has failed, partitioning the 10.0.1.0 subnet into two halves. However, because neither router is aware of the failure, they are both trying to forward all traffic destined to this subnet out their upper interface. Therefore, Router-A will not be able to reach Host-B and Router-B will not be able to communicate with Host-A.

In general, there are two simple and effective ways to fix this problem:

- Utilize a mixture of Layer 2 and Layer 3 (such as with "routing switches"/MLS)
- Place only a single Layer 2 switch between routers (as well as between the "switching router" forms of Layer 3 switches)

Under the first approach, MLS is used to create a Layer 2 environment that, because it is redundant, remains contiguous even after the failure of any single link. Figure 3-18 illustrates this approach.

Figure 3-18   *Avoiding Discontiguous Subnets With A Routing Switch (MLS)*

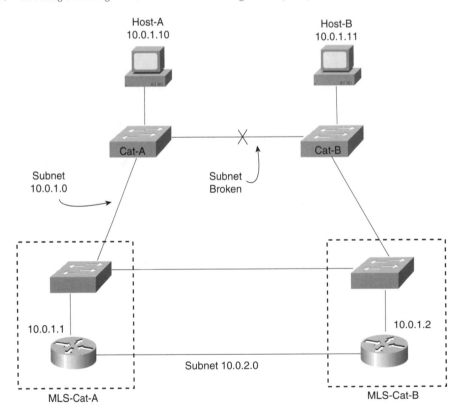

Figure 3-18 shows a logical representation of MLS devices where the Layer 2 and Layer 3 components are drawn separately in order to highlight the redundant Layer 2 configuration.

NOTE	The design in Figure 3-18 could also be implemented using switching router technology such as the Catalyst 8500s by utilizing bridging/IRB.

The second solution to the discontiguous subnet problem is to always use a single Layer 2 switch between routers, as shown in Figure 3-19.

Figure 3-19   *Avoiding Discontiguous Subnets By Using a Single Layer 2 Switch*

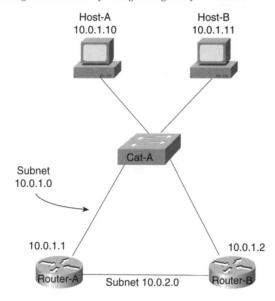

Because this eliminates the "chain" of Layer 2 switches shown in Figure 3-17, it allows any single link to fail without partitioning the subnet.

VTP

In some situations, the VLAN Trunking Protocol (VTP) can be useful for automatically distributing the list of VLANs to every switch in the campus. However, it is important to realize that this can automatically lead to campus-wide VLANs. Moreover, as discussed in Chapter 12 of *Cisco LAN Switching*, VTP can create significant network outages when it corrupts the global VLAN list.

When using VTP in large networks, consider overriding the default behavior using one of two techniques:

- VTP transparent mode
- Multiple VTP domains

First, many large networks essentially disable VTP by using the transparent mode of the protocol (there is no **set vtp disable** command). When using VTP transparent mode, you have absolute control over which VLANs are configured on each switch. This can allow you to prune back VLANs where they are not required to optimize your network.

Second, when organizations do decide to utilize VTP server and client mode, it is often beneficial to use a separate VTP domain name for each distribution block. This provides several benefits:

- It breaks the default behavior of spreading every VLAN to every switch (in other words, campus-wide VLANs).
- It constrains VTP problems to a single building.
- It allows the VTP protocol to better mirror the multilayer model.
- It can reduce Spanning Tree overhead.

Passwords

Because the XDI/CatOS-interface Catalysts (currently this includes 4000s, 5000s, and some 6000 configurations) automatically allow access by default, be sure to set user and privilege mode passwords. In addition, be certain to change the default SNMP community strings (unlike the routers, SNMP is enabled by default on XDI/CatOS-interface Catalysts).

Port Configurations

When configuring ports, especially important trunk links, hard-code as many parameters as possible. For example, relying on 10/100 speed and duplex negotiation protocols has been shown to occasionally fail. In addition, the state (**on** or **off**) and type (**isl** or **802.1Q**) of your Ethernet trunks should be hard-coded.

TIP   One exception to this rule concerns the use of PAgP, the Port Aggregation Protocol used to negotiate EtherChannel links. If PagP is hard-coded to the **on** state, this prevents the Catalyst from performing some value-added processing that can help in certain situations such as Spanning Tree failover.

Review Questions

This section includes a variety of questions on the topic of campus design implementation. By completing these, you can test your mastery of the material included in this chapter as well as help prepare yourself for the CCIE written and lab tests.

1 This chapter mentioned many advantages to using the multilayer model. List as many as possible.

2 This chapter also mentioned many disadvantages to using campus-wide VLANs. List as many as possible.

3 List some of the issues concerning management VLAN design.

4 What are some factors to be considered when determining where to place Root Bridges?

5 List five techniques that are available for campus load balancing.

6 What is the primary difference between using routing switches (MLS) and switching routers in MDF/distribution layer devices?

7 What are the pros and cons of using ATM?

INDEX

Numerics

5/3/1 rule, 8
80/20 rule, 13, 25
8500s
    HSRP, load balancing, 96
    MDF switches, 46–48
    MLS, 48–49
    practical applications, 99
    restricting STP, 84

A

access layer closets, 32, 113
access lists, Layer 3, 35
addresses (Layer 3), summarizing, 35
applications, enterprise databases, 25
architecture (client/server), affect on server
    resources, 25
ARP (Address Resolution Protocol), frames, 9
ATM (Asynchronous Transfer Mode)
    backbone, reachability, 103–104
    core, extending, 104
    Ethernet links, 103–104
    LANE
        BUS placement, 105
        SSRP, 104
    load balancing, 97
    MPOA (Multiprotocol over ATM), 105–106
    NSAP addresses, 106
    practical applications, 101–102

B

backbone (ATM), reachability, 103–104
BackboneFast, enabling, 92
bandwidth
    bridged LANs, 12
    multilayer network model, 58
    shared media hubs, 37
    sharing, 7

bridging
    80/20 rule, 13
    bandwidth consumption, 12
    LANs, segmentation, 10–13
broadcasts
    ARP frames, 9
    bandwidth consumption, 12
    domains, 14, 17–18
BUS (Broadcast and Unknown Server),
    placement, 105

C

cabling
    IDF (Intermediate Distribution Frame), 26–28
        access layer, 32
        hubs, 28
        Layer 2 Vs, 81
        reliability, 28
        requirements, 27–28
    MDF (Main Distribution Frame), 29
        distribution layer, 32
        high availability, 30
        Layer 2 switches, 30
        Layer 2 triangles, 81
        MLS switches, 31
        redundancy, 29
        requirements, 30
        VTP domains, 57
campus networks
    80/20 rule, 25
    ATM, practical applications, 101–102
    core layer, 33, 76
    designing
        campus-wide VLANs model, 37–40
        multilayer model, 42–46
        requirements, 33
        router and hub model, 36–37
    discontiguous subnets, 113–115
    distribution layer, 113
    IDF (Intermediate Distribution Frame),
        26-28, 113

O

P-Q